Mary Frances Whitney

C. PETER WAGNER

APOSTLES *and* PROPHETS
THE FOUNDATION OF THE CHURCH

Regal

A Division of Gospel Light
Ventura, California, U.S.A.

Published by Regal Books
A Division of Gospel Light
Ventura, California, U.S.A.
Printed in the U.S.A.

Regal Books is a ministry of Gospel Light, an evangelical Christian publisher
dedicated to serving the local church. We believe God's vision for Gospel Light
is to provide church leaders with biblical, user-friendly materials that will help
them evangelize, disciple and minister to children, youth and families.

It is our prayer that this Regal book will help you discover biblical truth for your
own life and help you meet the needs of others. May God richly bless you.

For a free catalog of resources from Regal Books/Gospel Light, please call your Christian supplier or contact us at 1-800-4-GOSPEL *or* www.regalbooks.com.

Cover and Interior Design by Rob Williams
Edited by Kyle Duncan

LIBRARY OF CONGRESS CATALOGING-IN-PUBLICATION DATA

Wagner, C. Peter.
    Apostles and prophets / C. Peter Wagner.
    p. cm.
    Includes bibliographical references.
    ISBN 0-8307-2574-1 (hardcover)
    ISBN 0-8307-2576-8 (paperback)
    1. Apostolate (Christian theology) 2. Apostles. 3. Prophets.
    4. Christian leadership. I. Title.

BV601.2 .W34 2000
262'.1 —dc21   00-042507

1 2 3 4 5 6 7 8 9 10 11 12 13 14 15 / 10 09 08 07 06 05 04 03 02 01 00

Rights for publishing this book in other languages are contracted by Gospel Literature
International (GLINT). GLINT also provides technical help for the adaptation, translation and publishing of Bible study resources and books in scores of languages worldwide. For further information, contact GLINT, P.O. Box 4060, Ontario, CA 91761-1003,
U.S.A. You may also send e-mail to Glintint@aol.com, or visit their website at
www.glint.org.

CONTENTS

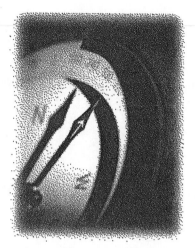

Chapter One

THE CHURCH'S ONE FOUNDATION

What is the foundation of the Church?

One of the best-known traditional hymns, sung across almost all denominational lines, is "The Church's One Foundation Is Jesus Christ Her Lord." It is easy to see why the author of this song would affirm that Jesus is the foundation of the Church. After all, it *is* His Church. He founded it. Jesus said, "I will build *My* Church." For many, to suggest that Jesus Christ might not be the foundation of the Church could be considered borderline heresy. So, in a broad and irrefutable sense, I want to affirm that Jesus certainly is the Church's foundation.

Once we agree on that theological truth, however, we must move from there to its practical implementation in our world today. Jesus not only founded the Church, but He also built into it a dynamic for ongoing expansion and development. He later gave us a revelation that He wanted his followers to see Him as the *cornerstone* of the Church that He would be building through the centuries, but that His design for a *foundation* was apostles and prophets.

A FOUNDATION OF APOSTLES AND PROPHETS

These truths regarding the foundation of the Church were revealed through the Apostle Paul in Ephesians 2:20: "[The household of God has been] built on the foundation of the apostles and prophets, Jesus Christ Himself being the chief cornerstone."

We may wonder why Jesus would put this strategic design in place for the Church. I think the most obvious reason is that He knew He would not be here in person to directly implement—or help execute—the building of His Church here on Earth.

In preparing his apostles for His departure, Jesus first assured them that His leaving would actually be to their *advantage*. When Peter first heard this news, he was so upset that he got into an argument with the Master. It must have been pretty intense, because that is when Jesus said to Peter, "Get behind Me, Satan!" (Matt. 16:23). Later when things calmed down, Jesus explained: "It is to your advantage that I go away; for if I do not go away, the Helper will not come to you; but if I depart, I will send Him to you" (John 16:7). The "Helper," of course, is the Holy Spirit.

This was profound. Essentially, Jesus was telling His disciples that the immediate presence of the Third Person of the Trinity would be more important to them than the immediate presence of the Second Person of the Trinity for the purpose of building

His Church. But where is the immediate presence of the Holy Spirit located? In every believer who has been filled with the Holy Spirit. So, while Jesus is omniscient and omnipresent and is always the head of the Church, He is now building His Church—as He has been doing for 2,000 years—through men and women who are empowered to do so by the Holy Spirit.

APOSTLES AND PROPHETS ARE GIFTS FROM JESUS

To be certain that His Church would be supplied with its proper foundation, Jesus gave gifts to the Church when He ascended into heaven from Earth. The Bible says, "'When He ascended on high, He led captivity captive, and gave gifts to men.' And He Himself gave some to be apostles, some prophets, some evangelists, and some pastors and teachers" (Eph. 4:8,11).

When I was in seminary, I was taught that the apostles and prophets were given only to get the Church started in the first century. After that time, they were no longer needed. My professors presumed that when the New Testament was completed and accepted by the Church, the foundational role of apostles and prophets was completed. Therefore, they stressed, all biblical references to apostles and prophets should be understood as a historical record rather than suggesting a contemporary reality.

In fact, until recently, most of the Protestant Church in general has operated under this assumption. Most of us were comfortable with pastors, so we had no problem calling someone "Pastor So-and-So." Teachers were okay. Like many others, I am sometimes referred to as "Dr." or "Professor" Wagner, signifying that I have been duly recognized as a teacher. We frequently speak of "Evangelist" Billy Graham or "Evangelist" Luis Palau as a matter of course. But to address an individual as "Apostle So-and-So" or "Prophet So-and-So" is considered by many Christian leaders to be, at best, inappropriate and, at worst, heretical.

This is curious because among those who hold this position are many who profess to have a very high view of biblical inspiration and authority. Yet it does not seem logical to draw some exegetical line between apostles and prophets on the one hand and evangelists, pastors and teachers on the other. It seems that such an interpretation could reflect a view of 60 percent biblical accuracy instead of 100 percent.

Furthermore, to postulate that apostles and prophets were needed for only a century or so is to sidestep the implications of the rest of the sentence that begins in Ephesians 4:11. The last words establish a specific time frame for the operation of these five gifts: "Till we all come to the unity of the faith and of the knowledge of the Son of God, to a perfect man, to the measure of the stature of the fullness of Christ" (Eph. 4:13). Very few, if any, Christian leaders I know would claim that the Body of Christ has reached the stage of perfection described here. And if this is the case, it would follow that there is still a need for apostles and prophets in the Church.

This helps us greatly to understand why God would tell us that the Church's foundation is "apostles and prophets, Jesus Christ Himself being the chief cornerstone" (Eph. 2:20).

FIRST APOSTLES

Not only do apostles and prophets constitute the foundation of the Church, but it is also biblical to state them in that specific order: apostles first and prophets second. This is found in one of the great chapters on spiritual gifts, 1 Corinthians 12: "And God has appointed these in the church: first apostles, second prophets" (v. 28). To my knowledge, this is the only place in the Bible where some of the spiritual gifts are listed in a specific sequence. When seen in conjunction with the other Scriptures that tell us apostles and prophets are the foundation of the Church, it makes perfect sense. What other gifts could possibly precede the foundational gifts?

This seems so elementary to me now, that I marvel at the fact that for generations we have been running our churches in reverse order (i.e., as if pastors, teachers and evangelists were the foundation). I say "we" because until recently I was as much a part of that mind-set as anyone else. The Church has actually functioned this way, and it has in fact done some remarkable things for the kingdom of God. But I also suppose that one could actually drive an automobile in reverse gear from Toledo to Cincinnati. It is possible, and the distance could eventually be covered, but no one does this. A car traveling for such a distance in reverse gear is obviously not operating as it was designed to operate. As we begin this twenty-first century, I believe it would be better to shift the Church into forward gear and even into overdrive!

Just think. If God, through a Church that had things backward, could evangelize practically the whole world, imagine what is in store for us now that we are getting things in order!

TEACHERS AND ADMINISTRATORS

The sequence continues in 1 Corinthians 12:28: "third teachers, after that miracles, then gifts of healings, helps, administrations, varieties of tongues." Let us focus on teachers, the third in order, and on administrators, who are listed later in the verse without a specific number.

When it comes right down to it, we have to admit that even a cursory analysis reveals that, for the most part, Christian churches are being run by administrators and teachers.

Traditional Christianity is largely structured around denominations, and most denominational executives are administrators—many of them excellent administrators. Thus, day after day and year after year, administrators are those who make decisions that affect the life and ministry of the churches under their jurisdiction. There is, of course, nothing wrong with administrators. The Bible teaches that they are necessary for churches to function as they should. But administrators will only do all they are supposed to do if they work under apostles and prophets.

Many recognize that a large number of Christian organizations that flourish in the first generation of leadership tend to lose some of their initial vigor after their founders pass off the scene. One reason is that the founder was very likely an apostle who exercised apostolic leadership in the organization, whether or not the term "apostle" was ever used. But when the apostle goes, more often than not the replacement turns out to be an administrator. There is a vast difference between an apostle and an administrator. While a few leaders have the ability to bridge that gap, the great majority do not.

If administrators have been running the churches translocally, teachers have been running the churches locally. Ever since the sermon became the focal point of the worship service, the pastor of the local church has been expected to be a teacher. Some pastors are known to spend 20 hours a week or more preparing their next sermon. Some leaders stress the teaching element so strongly that they take their argument one step further. They argue that in Ephesians 4:11, "pastors and teachers" should not be understood as two separate offices, but that they should be combined into one pastor-teacher office. I do not agree with this conclusion. The point remains, however, that our local churches have largely been led by teachers. It has been a difficult period because, in reality, most traditional churches do not see their pastor-teachers as leaders but, rather, as employees.

Researcher George Barna agrees: "As long as the Church persists in being led by teachers, it will flounder. Identifying, developing, deploying and supporting gifted *leaders* will renew the vision, energy, and impact of the Church."[1] New apostolic churches typically have pastors who are primarily leaders, most of whom also teach well. This is a very significant difference in emphasis.

No wonder some today have difficulty with the suggestion that the foundation of the Church is apostles and prophets. They have always thought that the foundation of the Church should be administrators and teachers!

Fortunately, important changes are rapidly taking place. As I view trends, I can clearly observe that these changes are taking place at a crucial time, just when the Church has moved into the third millennium.

A SPRINGBOARD TO THE TWENTY-FIRST CENTURY

One of the privileges of our generation has been to watch the transition from the twentieth century to the twenty-first century and thereby from the second millennium to the third millennium after Christ. Extraordinary things have been happening as we have crossed the line. I believe that God prepared the Church for this transition by raising up apostles in the 1990s. To use a visual analogy, I see apostles as having taken off from a "springboard" to make the leap for the Church and to carry us into this new century.

The springboard itself was set in place before the twentieth century began. By scanning history we can identify the major components of what I am calling the springboard.

Sixteenth Century: Reformed Theology

The apostolic move into the twenty-first century is not calling for radical adjustments in theology. Across the spectrum there is widespread agreement on the basic tenets of theology. These bulwark precepts were set in place during the Reformation of the sixteenth century by Martin Luther, John Calvin and others. Reformed theology includes three major theological convictions that most church leaders consider non-negotiable:

The authority of Scripture. In all matters of Christian faith and practice, the Bible is the final authority. Few leaders of vital, evangelical, life-giving churches are inclined to call this into question. Those segments of Christianity that do raise questions about biblical inspiration have, by and large, become so weak that they have all but forfeited the role of pacesetters for our new century.

Justification by faith. In Martin Luther's sixteenth century Germany, the Roman Catholic Church was teaching that people could get to heaven only by doing good works and participating in the sacraments. If they could afford them, many people were also buying so-called indulgences from the Church in order to shorten the time they would have to spend in purgatory to atone for their sins. Christian people, if asked, had no way of knowing for sure whether or not they would go to heaven because they never knew if they had been good enough. The Reformers clearly saw that the blood shed by Jesus on the cross was all that was needed to atone for sins and that faith in Jesus Christ as personal Savior was the only requirement for eternal life. As Bible-believing Christians, we all continue to agree with this today.

The priesthood of all believers. When we are born again into the family of God, God becomes our Father. Jesus taught us to pray, "Our Father . . ." Before the Reformation, however, Christians were taught that they were not worthy to approach God directly, but rather that they needed to approach Him through a duly authorized priest or through Mary and the saints. For four centuries since the Reformation, true believers have not doubted that they can go to God directly on their own initiative and also that God greatly enjoys it when they do.

Eighteenth Century: Wesleyan Holiness

In the eighteenth century, John Wesley was used by God to bring some very important new emphases into the Body of Christ. He did not question the three foundational doctrines listed above, but he did question some of the other rigid theological conclusions of the Reformers. Part of the fresh air Wesley brought to Christianity was his view that Christians could actually be holy and live holy lives, just as God is holy. Reformed theology taught that while believers should constantly strive to be more and more holy, none will actually achieve holiness in this life because only God is holy.

I am fully aware that many godly churches today still hold the Reformed doctrine of sanctification; that is one reason why I would not call a certain view of holiness a nonnegotiable, as I do the three theological convictions above. However, I do feel that holiness is a part of the springboard from which apostles are leading us into the twenty-first century. I am convinced that the churches on the cutting edges of what God is doing here in the new millennium will be churches that teach and practice bona fide holiness. I expand on this greatly in my book *Radical Holiness for Radical Living*, which I recommend to all who desire to be counted as pacesetters in the Church.

Nineteenth Century: The Modern Missionary Movement

Surprisingly, the churches of the sixteenth, seventeenth and eighteenth centuries were not strong missionary churches. Many historians of missions date the beginning of the modern missionary movement with William Carey's ministry in India, beginning in the 1790s. Since then, however, the worldwide expansion of the Christian movement has been remarkable. There has been no diminishment of the burning desire of believers to fulfill Christ's Great Commission to make disciples of every people group in the world. Today we are fortunate to belong to the first generation of Christians for whom there is light at the end of the Great Commission tunnel.

The apostolically oriented churches that will be moving the Body of Christ forward in this twenty-first century have aggressive missionary outreach in their spiritual DNA. An aggressive missionary mind-set is an established part of the springboard from which the apostles are taking us forward today.

THE MAJOR STEPS THROUGH THE TWENTIETH CENTURY

Let us say, then, that the major elements of the springboard were in place as the twentieth century began. Throughout the last century, several subsequent steps were taken to advance us to the end of the springboard, at which time apostles began to be recognized and encouraged and we were therefore ready for the twenty-first century. Let us take a look at these milestone movements from the twentieth century.

1900s: The Pentecostal Movement

In my view, it was quite prophetic that God chose to pour out His Holy Spirit on a group of worshippers in Topeka, Kansas, precisely on the New Year's Eve that transitioned us from the nineteenth century to the twentieth. The modern Pentecostal Movement was born then and it received a greater spark a few years later in the famous Azusa Street Revival.

This first step out onto the springboard in the twentieth century—and toward the twenty-first century—essentially brought the Third Person of the Trinity from relative obscurity into the mainstream of Church life. The sixteenth century Reformers had reestablished God as a Father whom we all could approach directly without the aid of a priest. The Wesleyans had refocused attention on the Son in highlighting our need to be more Christlike in our daily living. The Pentecostals recovered the immediate presence and availability of the Holy Spirit in the lives and ministries of all believers. So with a more complete understanding of the practical outworking of the Trinity in place, God was then poised to move the Body of Christ to new levels.

Progress did not happen immediately, however. Negative reactions on the part of traditional Christians, especially to the phenomenon of speaking in tongues, caused serious divisions that persisted until the middle of the century. In recent years, however, the work of the Holy Spirit in power ministries, healings, deliverance, prophecy, miracles, ecstatic experiences and the like is becoming quite broadly accepted across the theological spectrum. The doctrine of secessionism that opposes such spiritual phenomena is attracting a rapidly diminishing number of proponents. Even those who do not often practice the presence of the Holy Spirit rarely deny the Spirit's value and validity for the kingdom of God.

The 1950s: Evangelism

Because of the unfortunate opposition to the Pentecostal Movement early in our century, it was not until around 1950 that God set out in place the second step out on the diving board toward the twenty-first century. At that time a strong movement for aggressive evangelism began, and it has increased in intensity ever since.

Evangelism took root among the Pentecostal segment of the Body of Christ with the rise of the so-called healing evangelists, represented by the likes of Oral Roberts and Gordon Lindsay. Billy Graham was the most highly visible representative of the Evangelical segment of the Body of Christ. Since the 1950s the roster of public evangelists has expanded greatly.

Following World War II, the number of Americans who gave their lives to launch out in foreign missions increased dramatically. They were led by GIs who had spent time in foreign lands and who had received a strong call to return to them with the gospel. Now that Third World churches are also sending out foreign missionaries in large numbers, the evangelistic force for our new century has a stronger base than ever before.

The 1960s: Compassion for the Poor and Oppressed

During the 1960s the Spirit began speaking strongly to the churches about our responsibility to reach out in a meaningful way to those less fortunate than we. Christian social responsibility, already present in some segments of the Church, began to become widespread. Some glitches occurred when certain ones attempted to advocate the unbiblical theology of liberation. Today it is a fact, however, that churches across the board are feeding hungry people, housing homeless people and standing up for social justice and righteousness more than ever before.

It was very important to take this step to prepare for what God wanted to do with His people in the twenty-first century.

The 1970s: A Great Prayer Movement

The great global prayer movement that has carried us into the twenty-first century had its beginnings in the 1970s. Few of the dynamic prayer ministries that we are so familiar with have roots preceding 1970. In fact:

- The 1970s saw the planting of the seeds of prayer.
- The 1980s saw the budding of prayer.
- The 1990s saw the blossoming of prayer.
- Today we are in the time of the fruit of prayer.

A good part of my personal involvement in the springboard toward the twenty-first century has been in this area of prayer. During the 1990s I coordinated the AD2000 United Prayer Track and the International Spiritual Warfare Network, authored the six-volume Prayer Warrior series, and my wife, Doris, and I joined Ted Haggard in founding the World Prayer Center of Colorado Springs. The vision for this center was to mobilize prayer worldwide by providing a central hub—or "switchboard"—where intercessors worldwide could be linked together for the gathering and disseminating of strategic prayer requests and needs. Just as my ministry in the 1990s was heavily focused on prayer, so too the Church shifted its sight onto prayer. The Body of Christ is now tooled for prayer to a greater degree than ever before in its history.

One of the most significant developments connected to the prayer movement has been the emergence of the office of intercessor. It was only in the 1980s that certain individuals began to be recognized as having a special spiritual gift of intercession. Intercessors have been around wherever life-giving churches existed, but their specialized ministry was largely hidden and thereby restricted. This is no longer the case. It is now not unusual these days to go into a given church and to have one of their church members introduced as "one of our intercessors" or "the leader of our prayer ministry" or even "our pastor of prayer."

Some may observe that "intercessor" is not an office listed in Ephesians 4:11 along with apostles, prophets, evangelists, pastors and teachers. I think that the reason for this is that intercessor is not a governmental gift but rather a catalytic gift. While Scripture does not specifically delineate the gift and office intercessor, I have argued in places like my book *Prayer Shield* that it is a legitimate spiritual gift.

A number of churches distinguish their intercessors by special name badges so that those who have special prayer needs know whom to approach for help. Intercessors constitute one of the three major offices, along with apostles and prophets, that are now recognized and that will equip us to serve God more effectively through our new century.

The 1980s: The Office of Prophet

A generation or two ago, certain segments of the Body of Christ began recognizing the office of prophet in their midst. But by and large, these segments were isolated from the mainstream. It was only in the 1980s that prophets began to be accepted by a wider spectrum of the Church. Of the three key offices of prophet, apostle and intercessor, it was more difficult for traditional Christians to feel comfortable with prophets than with the other two offices. A strong mind-set of skepticism prevailed among many leaders who believed that once God spoke to us through the Bible, no further revelation was necessary. The idea that God still speaks important things to us today, either through prophets or otherwise, actually has been considered heresy by some.

The significant role of prophets as a foundation for the Body of Christ for our new century is one of the principal themes of the rest of this book.

The 1990s: The Office of Apostle

With the recognition of the office of apostle in the 1990s, the complete government of the Church came into place for the first time since the early centuries. I am aware that some may question that statement. One of the reasons for this is the fact that in all probability, there has never been a time in Church history when the Church has been without apostles. I agree. That is why I use the terms "the recognition" of the "office" of apostle, not "the establishment" of what we could call "apostolic function." These nuances will become clearer in later chapters.

Others would correctly point out that in certain segments of the Church the office of apostle has, indeed, been recognized throughout the past two millennia. The Roman Catholic Church, the Anglican or Episcopal Church and many denominations that have actually incorporated "apostolic" into their name would come to mind as examples. However, just as was true of prophetic movements, the emphases of these apostolic movements had not penetrated the mainstream of what I am calling life-giving evangelical churches that now are the cutting edge of the spread of Christianity. This only began to happen in the 1990s.

The production of thoughtful and informative books has aided in the rapidly expanding acceptance of apostles and true apostolic ministry in the beginning of this century. Many more will be forthcoming, but at this writing I highly recommend four books on apostles and apostolic ministry:

- *Apostles and the Emerging Apostolic Movement* by David Cannistraci. At the present time, this is the best overall textbook on the most essential concepts for understanding biblically and practically what apostles are and what they do. This book is a good starting point for those who want to get into the subject.
- *Apostles, Prophets and the Coming Moves of God* by Bishop Bill Hamon. Bill Hamon of Christian International has been an inside player in the development of apostolic ministries for much longer than most other evangelical leaders. Better than any other book, this one provides a historical context for what is happening in the movement. It is very informative.
- *Moving in the Apostolic* by John Eckhardt. John Eckhardt, an inner-city apostle in Chicago, is more fired up than most with the excitement of actually ministering with an apostolic anointing. His book is the most motivational of the four. When you read it, you will love apostles!
- *End Time Warriors* by John Kelly and Paul Costa. Many would agree that John Kelly is the most articulate

spokesperson on the scene today for the nuts and bolts of apostolic ministry. His book will help raise your understanding of contemporary apostles to a new level.

The Jump into a New Century

What I have been calling the New Apostolic Reformation seemed to come into its own by the end of the 1990s. For several years I have been using the following definition for this movement:

The New Apostolic Reformation is an extraordinary work of God at the close of the twentieth century which is, to a significant extent, changing the shape of Protestant Christianity around the world. For almost 500 years Christian churches have largely functioned within traditional denominational structures of one kind or another. Particularly in the 1990s, but with roots going back for almost a century, new forms and operational procedures are now emerging in areas such as local church government, interchurch relationships, financing, evangelism, missions, prayer, leadership selection and training, the role of supernatural power, worship and other important aspects of church life. Some of these changes are being seen within denominations themselves, but for the most part they are taking the form of loosely structured apostolic networks. In virtually every region of the world, these new apostolic churches constitute the fastest growing segment of Christianity.

In a word, we are now experiencing what is clearly the most radical change in the way of doing church since the Protestant

Reformation. I might go a bit further to even suggest that this could possibly be an even more radical change than the Reformation. The change in the time of the Reformation was largely theological, with some minimal changes in congregational life. The New Apostolic Reformation is largely a change in congregational life, with minimal adjustments in theology. That is why I said that it was a change in the way of "doing church."

Just as we have the beginnings of a useful body of literature on the gift and office of apostle, we also have good sources for the New Apostolic Reformation. These are the three books that I most recommend at the present time:

- *Reinventing American Protestantism* by Donald E. Miller. Sociologist of religion Donald Miller undertook an extensive study of three movements that were among the pioneers of the New Apostolic Reformation in America: Vineyard, Calvary Chapel and Hope Chapel. This is not a dull book on sociology, but an extremely informative description and analysis of these dynamic prototypes. There is no other book quite like it.
- *The New Apostolic Churches* edited by C. Peter Wagner. As I moved into my research on the New Apostolic Reformation, I had the privilege of building personal relationships with several of the movement's top apostolic leaders. In this book I do an introductory chapter, and then 18 apostles contribute first-person chapters on their own movements. I call this the "catalog" of the New Apostolic Reformation.
- *Churchquake!* by C. Peter Wagner. This is my 71,000-word textbook on the New Apostolic Reformation. If you feel that you have time to read only one of the

seven books I am recommending here, this is the book I would suggest for the overall picture.

Ready to Move Ahead

The New Apostolic Reformation could not have materialized without the springboard—and without the various steps along the springboard—during the past century. A major reason is that the foundation of the Church needed to be in place before God could begin to do all He wants to do in our new millennium.

To reiterate, the foundation of the Church is apostles and prophets, with Jesus Christ being the chief cornerstone. Now let us look at what this might mean for us and our churches.

Note
1. George Barna, "The Second Coming of the Church," *Enrichment* (winter 2000), p. 18 (emphasis mine).

Chapter Two

WHAT APOSTLES HAVE

What makes apostles different from other members of the Body of Christ? This question almost always comes up when I enter into a conversation about the New Apostolic Reformation. Generally, the tone behind the question is not one of opposition to the idea that there might be apostles in the Church today, but rather a sincere desire for information. Actually, there has been much less criticism forthcoming on this subject than I had anticipated.

Not that debate is absent. Much stimulating discussion is being carried on both verbally and in print, as would be expected when a new concept like this is being introduced. Iron is sharpening iron. But the nature of most of the discussion is not adversarial, although some people, unfortunately, have indeed labeled this movement as heresy. For the most part, however, the dialogue reflects a mutual desire to hear clearly what the

Spirit is saying to the churches.

I believe there are two important characteristics that set apostles apart from other members of the Body of Christ: the *authority* of apostles and the *spheres* of apostolic authority. Let us look at them one at a time.

APOSTLES HAVE UNUSUAL AUTHORITY

In my book *Churchquake!* I say:

> Of all the radical changes in the New Apostolic Reformation, I regard one of them as the most radical of all. It is so important that I have chosen these words very carefully: *The amount of spiritual authority delegated by the Holy Spirit to individuals.*[1]

The two operative words in this statement are "authority" and "individuals."

Until recently the central focus of authority in our churches existed in groups, not in individuals. Trust has been placed in sessions, consistories, nominating committees, deacon boards, trustees, congregations, presbyteries, associations, general councils, cabinets, conventions, synods and the like. Rarely has trust for ultimate decision making been given to individuals such as pastors or apostles. This, however, is changing decisively in the New Apostolic Reformation.

Much information about apostles surfaces in 1 and 2 Corinthians. Among the believers in Corinth, certain factions had determined to undermine Paul's apostolic leadership over their church. Therefore, when Paul writes his epistles to that church, he opens his heart on many things that we might not have discovered had he not been so upset. I will quote quite a bit from the Corinthian letters in this section.

As a starter, Paul finds it necessary to assert his apostolic authority by writing: "For even if I should boast somewhat more about our *authority*, which the Lord gave us for edification and not for your destruction, I shall not be ashamed" (2 Cor. 10:8, emphasis mine). Unquestionably, Paul had unusual authority. However, the next question is: Where did this authority come from?

Paul's authority as an apostle came from the same sources that provide today's apostles with their extraordinary authority. I see five principal sources of apostolic authority; every bona fide apostle will score high on these five components.

1. APOSTLES HAVE A SPIRITUAL GIFT

Why some should attempt to deny that there is such a thing as a spiritual gift of apostle escapes me, but they do. One of the major New Testament chapters on spiritual gifts is 1 Corinthians 12. This is where we learn that "God has set the members, each one of them, in the body just as He pleased" (1 Cor. 12:18). Spiritual gifts determine precisely what particular function each one of us has in the Body of Christ, and God is the one who chooses which gift or gifts we should have.

Many different spiritual gifts are discussed in 1 Corinthians 12. One of those gifts is the gift of apostle. In verse 28 Paul asserts that in the Church, apostles are first and prophets second (as I mentioned in the last chapter). In verse 29, Paul goes on to ask the rhetorical question, "Are all apostles?" The answer is obviously no, but just as obviously the implication is that some *are* apostles. I have heard arguments against regarding apostles as a gift in this particular text, but these arguments do not subsequently explain why teaching or administrating or performing miracles or speaking in tongues or helping should not be considered gifts as well, even though they are listed in the same verse. The best interpretation, in my opinion, accepts the gift of apostle along with the other spiritual gifts.

God determines who should receive what gift. This is why when Paul asserts that he is a bona fide apostle in 2 Corinthians 10:8 (the verse we looked at above), he speaks of his authority *"which the Lord gave us"* (emphasis mine). No apostolic authority is self-generated. It comes only as God chooses to delegate it.

A commonly used sociological term for apostles, introduced by Max Weber, is "charismatic leaders." "Charismatic" in this secular sense does not refer to spiritual gifts, but rather to an extraordinary degree of authority inherent in the leader. It is what John Maxwell calls "The Law of E. F. Hutton" in his book *The 21 Irrefutable Laws of Leadership*. When the leader speaks, people listen. I like the description of apostles that I once heard from Jack Whitesell: "Apostles are leaders of great magnitude."

The apostle does not gain authority by attaining a title or by being awarded a hierarchical position. Rather, we are talking about a *spiritual* authority conferred by God Himself. But when God chooses to confer it, and when this authority is recognized both by the apostle and by those around the apostle, this authority is unusual to say the least.

2. APOSTLES HAVE AN ASSIGNMENT, OR CALL

Earlier in 1 Corinthians 12 we read: "There are diversities of gifts, but the same Spirit. There are differences of ministries, but the same Lord. And there are diversities of activities, but it is the same God who works all in all" (vv. 4-6). If all apostles have the *gift* of apostle as I argued above, all do not have the same *ministries* or the same *activities*. Not all apostles are called to do the same thing.

A little later on, I want to describe some of the more important varieties of apostolic ministries. My purpose here, however, is simply to point out that when a given apostle knows for sure exactly what ministry or call God has given him or her, their self-confidence rises accordingly. This is not pride. Their confidence rests not in their own ability but in a deep assurance that they are obeying God and acting according to His will. To the degree that this happens, the apostle's authority increases.

3. APOSTLES HAVE EXTRAORDINARY CHARACTER

I have chosen the phrase "extraordinary character" very carefully. I do not mean it as a moralizing admonition that apostles should shape up and behave themselves better in order to prove that they might be bona fide apostles. What I mean is that God will not entrust genuine apostolic authority to individuals who have not already attained extraordinary character. There is no such thing as an average apostle. While no apostles are perfect and while all of them have plenty of room for improvement both inwardly and outwardly, all apostles are considerably above average.

For example, at one point Paul writes to the Philippians about sending Timothy to them, a member of his apostolic team, to set things in order there. To help open the door for

Timothy's apostolic ministry in Philippi, Paul headlines his principal qualifier in these words: "But you know his proven *character*" (Phil. 2:22, emphasis mine).

Christian leaders have an awesome responsibility to live exemplary lives. James writes, "My brethren, let not many of you become teachers, knowing that we shall receive a stricter judgment" (Jas. 3:1). What this means is that God has a double standard for judgment: one standard for leaders and another for the rest of the Body of Christ.

It is interesting to observe that the New Testament contains no list of character or behavioral standards to gain or maintain membership in the Church except, of course, a profession of faith in Jesus as Savior and Lord. Some would suggest that baptism is a requirement and they can make a good biblical argument for their position. At the same time, however, many recognized segments of the Church, such as the Salvation Army or Methodists or Nazarenes or Congregationalists, hold baptism much more lightly, not regarding it as an absolute requirement for church membership.

Paul wrote 1 Corinthians to scold the believers in Corinth for violating a number of Christian character standards, but it is notable that he recommended excommunication for only one individual who persisted in sleeping with his stepmother (see 1 Cor. 5). Apparently the rest of the Corinthian Christians were allowed to maintain church membership while they were working on improving their character.

Apostles Must Be Blameless

Such leeway, however, is not true for leaders. Paul wrote letters to both Timothy and Titus, setting forth specific character requirements for church leaders—from deacons to elders to bishops. 1 Timothy 3 tells us that believers would not qualify as bishops, for example, unless they were mature ("not a novice," v. 6); serious ("sober-minded," v. 2); leading a functional family ("if a man does not know how to rule his own house, how will he take care of the church of God?," v. 5); living a modest lifestyle ("not greedy for money," v. 3); and, right at the top of the list, above reproach ("blameless," v. 2).

In order for apostles, who are regarded as first among Christian leaders (see 1 Cor. 12:28), to gain the high-ranking spiritual responsibility they are being given, they need to meet the standards for biblical leadership. They can identify with the apostle Paul, who, when answering the objections of some Corinthians to his apostolic authority, wrote: "For I know nothing against myself" (1 Cor. 4:4). These are remarkable words. But only on the basis of such a level of extraordinary character could Paul continue later in the same chapter to say, "Therefore I urge you, imitate me" (1 Cor. 4:16). True apostles can stand before their followers and say without hesitation, "Imitate me!"

Apostles Must Be Humble

Such a claim would be presumptuous if it were not clothed in humility. I believe that true humility is intentional. It is a choice. No one is born humble, as anyone who has been close to a three- or four- year-old well knows. Humility is learned, and apostles have learned how to be humble. They understand servant leadership. They know that Jesus said whoever humbles himself will be exalted (see Matt. 23:12). Note that the burden is on the leader to humble himself or herself. If leaders are not humble, they have no one to blame but themselves. If they fail in this area, God will not anoint them with apostolic authority.

A good bit of the authority of an apostle, therefore, comes from extraordinary character clothed in humility.

4. APOSTLES HAVE FOLLOWERS

It should go without saying that all apostles have followers. No followers, no apostle! The fact of the matter is, however, that some ambitious and misguided individuals assume the title of "apostle" prematurely. I have heard of some pastors who attend a conference on apostolic ministry and decide that it would be nice to be an apostle. They then return home and have business cards printed with the title "Apostle So-and-So," passing out their new cards at every opportunity. These are the ones who fit the term "self-appointed apostles."

Every true apostle has had his or her gift and office substantiated by a significant number of visible, mature leaders who have chosen to follow the apostle. By definition, an apostle is a leader of leaders. In most cases, the apostle heads up an apostolic network of pastors and other leaders who, with a certain amount of sanctified pride, do not hesitate to let others know they are under the authority of a given apostle. This is a public relationship that outsiders can observe, analyze, test and verify. True apostles are not self-appointed. In a real sense, they are appointed through the affirmation and the ongoing loyalty of their followers.

The followers submit voluntarily to the apostle; no one forces an individual to follow a given apostle. Apostolic networks are not denominational structures in which a pastor's credentials, status, call to a given church, salary level, promotions, retirement program, educational requirements and other personal and ministry considerations are determined by a legal structure. Pastors join and remain in a certain apostolic network because they want to be under the apostle. If at any time they feel they are no longer benefiting from their relationship with the apostle, they are free to leave. In most cases, the apostle will encourage them to do so, because discontented or disloyal followers will weaken the whole network.

This relationship works so well because it is a win-win situation that is extremely fulfilling to both the apostle and the follower. If we could take an X ray of the minds of the apostle and the follower, here is what we would find: The apostle is thinking, *How can I help this person be everything that God wants him to be?* (This is the true, driving motivation of an apostle.) And, as a result, the follower is thinking, *This apostle adds incredible value to my life and ministry!* This is, therefore, an unbeatable combination.

Personally, I have been involved in a good bit of apostolic ministry and can testify that the greatest accomplishments in my life are based upon what I have helped others to attain. I am well pleased with what God has done with so many of my students. I think of John Wimber, Rick Warren, Paul Rader, John Maxwell, Walt Kallestad, Kent Hunter, Elmer Towns and Cindy Jacobs, just to name a few.

For example, I remember that when Cindy Jacobs's first book, *Possessing the Gates of the Enemy*, was released, it literally gave me more pleasure than any of my own books that were released around that time. By saying this, I do not mean to imply that these individuals' careers would have been retarded or constrained if they had not paid tuition for my courses. Nevertheless, I do believe that each of them would tell you I had at least a small part to play in getting them to where they are today.

There is good biblical precedence for this type of loving apostolic relationship. The apostle Paul said to his followers in

Thessalonica that he was gentle with them "as a nursing mother cherishes her own children" (1 Thess. 2:7) and that he charged them "as a father does his own children" (1 Thess. 2:11). Then he went on to say, "What is our hope, or joy, or crown of rejoicing? Is it not even you in the presence of our Lord Jesus Christ at His coming?" (1 Thess. 2:19). The apostle John said, "I have no greater joy than to hear that my children walk in truth" (3 John 4). I know that this is authentic apostolic desire because I can personally identify with it. I love it when my investment in the lives and ministries of others pays off!

When this kind of mutual relationship develops between apostle and followers, it builds under the apostle a very secure base for exercising authority.

5. APOSTLES HAVE VISION

Apostles know where they are going. Not only that, but they know where the Church should be going. Where do they get this vision? They receive revelation from God.

In writing to the Corinthians, the apostle Paul said, "It is doubtless not profitable for me to boast. I will come to visions and revelations of the Lord" (2 Cor. 12:1). Then he told them the story of being taken into the third heaven and learning truths so awesome and profound that he could not even share them with others. He goes on to say that his notorious "thorn in the flesh" was given to him "lest I should be exalted above measure by the abundance of the revelations" that he constantly received from God (2 Cor. 12:7).

One of the major roles of an apostle is to communicate to the Church "what the Spirit says to the churches," as we see in the book of Revelation (see Rev. 2:7). The apostle knows what the Spirit is saying by receiving revelation from God. When this happens, authority increases exponentially; the apostle announces the word of the Lord. This is not the *logos* word contained in the canon of Scripture, which cannot be added to or subtracted from. Rather, it is the *rhema* word through which God gives us specific direction regarding His will for the present and future.

Apostles who receive the word of the Lord translate it into a concrete vision and announce to their followers that it is what the Spirit is saying to the churches for this time and place, thus opening the way for powerful ministry. If such apostles have heard accurately, their followers will confirm to them that the vision is valid and that they want to participate in seeing it fulfilled.

Two Ways to Receive Revelation

Revelation from God is communicated to apostles in two ways. One method is when the apostle, like the apostle Paul, receives the revelation directly. I have experienced such revelation myself from time to time, although I have never entered into the third heaven—or ever been close, to my knowledge! Just to be concrete for a moment, let me share an example of such direct revelation that occurred recently in my own life. The revelation I received had to do with the prayer assignment for the Body of Christ to the 40/70 Window.

In late 1999, Global Harvest Ministries (i.e., the nonprofit organization that Doris and I had formed in order to handle the affairs of the AD2000 United Prayer Track) was finishing the AD2000 Movement's 10-year assignment to concentrate our prayers on the 10/40 Window. For those who may not know, the 10/40 Window is the swath of earth that lies between the latitudes of 10 degrees and 40 degrees north of the equator and between the Atlantic and Pacific Oceans. This huge area includes the largest number of unreached peoples on the planet (including major parts of Africa, Asia, China, the Middle East and India).

The climax of our 10-year, 10/40 Window prayer assignment was the unparalleled four-hour, nonstop worship service held in the ancient amphitheater in Ephesus, Turkey, on October 1, 1999. No fewer than 5,000 believers from 62 nations joined their hearts and voices together, exalting the King of kings and the Lord of lords. We called it Celebration Ephesus.

Before and during the event, I honestly did not have the slightest idea how the focus of the global prayer movement would be directed in the future. To be truthful, I was exhausted and wanted to spend some time regrouping and taking it easy. As soon as I arrived back in the World Prayer Center in mid-October, however, many of the prayer leaders close to me began to admonish me rather relentlessly. "Without a vision, the people perish," they began to tell me.

Chuck Pierce summed it up by saying, "Peter, you are the apostle of the world prayer movement. You are the one responsible for casting the vision for all of us. If you do not seek the Lord for the next vision now, we are in danger of losing the momentum that God has given us for a whole decade." So much for my desired R & R!

Inquiring of the Lord

I did what I knew I had to do, which was to inquire of the Lord. I asked Him, "Lord, where do you want us to go in the future?" This was no 40-day—or even three-day—fast. As I recall, I spoke to God in the shower that morning, and after breakfast the revelation began, thick and fast. Before noon, I was certain that for the next five years God wanted us to concentrate on the 40/70 Window, which encompasses a gigantic chunk of the planet running from Iceland to the tip of Siberia.

I knew God wanted us to focus on that part of the world that contains, among other things, the largest number of non-born-again Christians on the face of the earth. As well, I knew that the principality of darkness most responsible for neutralizing the power of Christianity in that area was the Queen of Heaven. For the sake of brevity, I am not going to provide a detailed explanation of the Queen of Heaven, other than to say it is a powerful counterfeit spirit that operates within many of the world's major religions. (For more information on the Queen of Heaven, see my two books *Confronting the Queen of Heaven* and *The Queen's Domain*. The surprising thing to me was that before that day, I never had the slightest interest in or attraction to the 40/70 Window.

As I shared this experience with my Global Harvest Ministries staff, you would have thought I had lit a fireworks display! The immediate, high-voltage affirmation that this is truly what the Spirit is saying to the churches was incredible. In fact, their reaction was a bit overwhelming as far as I was concerned. From that moment, new information about the 40/70 Window started pouring into the Global Harvest Ministries office. Intercessor after intercessor began to feel fires of passion rise up in their spirits to pray for Europe, Eurasia, Russia, the Turkish Belt, Greece, Italy, Poland and numerous other places. Soon after I announced the vision, I was told that three of my personal intercessors had known for some time that we were to shift to the 40/70 Window, but God did not allow them to tell me.

I have told this story not to introduce information on the global prayer movement, but to illustrate firsthand how an apostle receives direct revelation from God. But the fact that some of my intercessors knew what God had in mind before I did points to the second way apostles receive revelation: namely, through prophets.

Apostles Hear Through Prophets

God can, and does, reveal His plans directly to apostles. But He also reveals His plans to prophets who, in turn, communicate them to apostles. Later I will go into considerable detail about how apostles and prophets must be hitched together in order to function as the foundation of the Church, so I will not elaborate much on it here. I will say, however, that I have been surprised to find that some apostles are not particularly inclined to team up with prophets. I think some apostles unnecessarily handicap themselves by not establishing close, working relationships with prophets.

How much revelation should be expected to come directly to the apostle and how much through prophets? At this point, I am not yet sure of the balance. My hunch is that this balance probably varies from apostle to apostle. In my case, I would say that a good bit more than half of the revelation I receive comes through prophets, a number of whom also serve Doris and me as personal intercessors. But I am sure that other apostles would have different reports as well.

In chapter 6, I will pick up on this issue of the apostle-prophet balance in regard to revelation. Meanwhile, I have tried to make the point that an apostle's propensity to hear from God (in whatever way) greatly increases the authority that is part and parcel of being a true apostle.

The authority of an apostle, in summary, does not derive from holding a position or title. It comes, pure and simple, from a divine anointing!

APOSTLES HAVE DETERMINED SPHERES

As I suggested at the beginning of the chapter, the two most distinguishing features of apostles, in my opinion, are the unusual *authority* they have and the *spheres* they are assigned. The bulk of this chapter has dealt with the authority of apostles and the sources from which that authority is derived. However, this second area of spheres is also extremely important, and I want to explain it briefly, but in high detail.

One of the reasons why Paul wrote to the Corinthians was to remind them, in no uncertain terms, that he was an apostle and that he had been given authority over them. In both of his letters to the Corinthians, Paul brings up the issue of spheres. The authority of an apostle is only operative within the sphere of ministry that God has assigned to the apostle. When apostles venture outside their appointed sphere of ministry, they have no more authority than any other member of the Body of Christ.

In 1 Corinthians Paul says, "Am I not an apostle? Am I not free? Have I not seen Jesus Christ our Lord? Are you not my work in the Lord? *If I am not an apostle to others, yet doubtless I am to you*" (1 Cor. 9:1,2, emphasis mine). What is Paul affirming here? He is saying, apparently, that he is not an apostle over the whole Church everywhere. And this was the case. Paul was not an apostle of Jerusalem or Rome or Alexandria. These regions were not his assigned apostolic spheres. But Corinth certainly was, as was Philippi and Ephesus and Lystra and Crete and other places.

By the time Paul writes 2 Corinthians, he is ready to elaborate a bit more on the matter of apostolic spheres. Chapter 10 has more detail on this subject than any other part of the Bible. He says, "We, however, will not boast beyond measure, but within the limits of the *sphere* which God appointed us—a *sphere* which especially includes you" (2 Cor. 10:13, emphasis mine).

Recognizing that apostolic ministry is not effective outside of designated spheres, Paul goes on to write, "For we are not overextending ourselves" (2 Cor. 10:14). Then when Paul suggests that he would go to the "regions beyond," he says that he would avoid "another man's sphere of accomplishment" (2 Cor. 10:16) and that he would not "build on another man's foundation" (Rom. 15:20).

VARIETIES OF APOSTOLIC SPHERES

When Paul wrote about apostolic spheres, he was referring to ecclesiastical spheres and geographical, or territorial, spheres. These are very common, but I have also observed that certain apostles have functional spheres as well. This gives us at least three approaches for accurately defining and describing apostolic spheres:

Ecclesiastical Spheres. These perhaps are the most common of all apostolic spheres. In them, apostles have authority over a certain number of churches and possibly their derivative ministries.

Functional Spheres. A functional sphere would include leaders in a certain arena of Christian ministry. For example, there might be an apostle over worship leaders who minister in a number of different churches. This apostle is not in a position of authority over churches, but over individuals with similar gifts and callings. This functional apostolic authority does not remove the need for worship leaders also to be under apostolic authority in the churches they represent. In other words, when functioning in their home sphere, the worship leader is under the authority of his or her church's apostolic authority (as opposed to the authority of the worship leader-apostle).

Geographical, or Territorial, Spheres. As we saw earlier, Paul's ecclesiastical sphere was also territorial. Functional spheres can also be territorial, such as an apostle of worship leaders in Spain who would not have the same authority over worship leaders in Germany.

It is important to recognize that these spheres are not necessarily mutually exclusive; I am not trying to put apostles in rigid boxes. What I am trying to do, however, is provide conceptual frameworks with corresponding terminology. Such defined frameworks will help us sort out what we are beginning to observe more frequently as the New Apostolic Reformation develops before our eyes, in order to understand better what God is beginning to do in this hour.

Note
1. C. Peter Wagner, *Churchquake!* (Ventura, CA: Regal Books, 1999), p. 75.

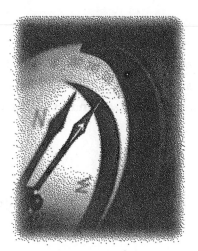

Chapter Three

HOW APOSTLES OPERATE

In 1999 when I wrote *Churchquake!* my textbook on the New Apostolic Reformation, I was aware that not all apostles were alike as far as their ministry assignments were concerned. The question had become quite clear to me: What are the different ministries or callings that apostles might typically have? However, when I wrote *Churchquake!* I still did not have the answer.

At the time, I did have what I considered a good definition for an apostle. I had originally written this definition more than 20 years ago in my 1979 book *Your Spiritual Gifts Can Help Your Church Grow*. When I began studying the apostolic movement in 1993, one of my pleasant surprises was that this definition seemed to hold up, even though I had written it before I knew very much about apostles. Here it is:

The gift of apostle is the special ability that God gives to certain members of the Body of Christ to assume and exercise general leadership over a number of churches with an extraordinary authority in spiritual matters that is spontaneously recognized and appreciated by those churches.[1]

NEEDED: ACCURATE TERMINOLOGY

Upon quoting this definition in *Churchquake!* I go on to say:

As I have continued to study the New Apostolic Reformation, however, it has become clear that this definition applies to many apostles, and perhaps the majority, but not to all apostles. I was hoping that by the time I finished this book I would have satisfactory terminology to name and define however many other kinds of apostles there might be. This has not happened as I wished, so we will simply leave the matter pending for further research.[2]

Not long after *Churchquake!* was published I had the "further research" I needed. The person who helped me more than anyone else was my friend Roger Mitchell from England. He had been an insider in apostolic networks long before I began to recognize their importance, working with Roger Forster in the Ichthus Movement and then starting his own network called Passion. It was from Roger Mitchell that I first heard the names "vertical apostle" and "horizontal apostle." This was, for me, what some call a eureka moment. It was so important that I remember when and where it happened: late October 1999, when I was sitting at a table in a hotel in Guatemala!

Let me explain.

In the last chapter I quoted 1 Corinthians 12, which says that we all have different gifts, ministries and activities. That was after I suggested that all true apostles have the spiritual gift of apostle, given to them by God and at His initiative. I briefly mentioned that apostles have their own individual calls, but now I want to be much more specific. All apostles have the same gift, but I now see that it is extremely helpful to distinguish four different *ministries* of apostles.

1. VERTICAL APOSTLES

Vertical apostles are the most common kind. These apostles typically head up an apostolic network consisting of a number of churches and sometimes include parachurch ministries as well. They have a specific sphere of influence and are the senior or lead apostle within that sphere. In this sense, their apostolic authority is defined and delineated (i.e., not broad based or horizontal) and does not typically extend outside their ministry sphere. The definition of the gift of apostle that I formulated back in 1979 describes vertical apostles. Many people today are like I was then, thinking that this is the *only* kind of apostle. In fact, when I wrote my book *The New Apostolic Churches*, inviting 18 apostles to contribute a chapter about their own movements, all 18 contributors were vertical apostles. A good bit of the literature we now have on the ministry of apostles still assumes that all apostles are vertical.

A major reason why we often assume that all apostles are vertical is because the apostle Paul, a role model for many, was a vertical apostle. He had a certain number of churches in his apostolic sphere, and he exercised apostolic authority within that sphere. Let me mention again what I brought up in the last chapter. Paul said to the Corinthians, "If I am not an apostle to others, yet doubtless I am to you" (1 Cor. 9:2). Paul knew that he was not an apostle to the whole Church. But, quite definitely, the church in Corinth was one of the churches within Paul's sphere as a vertical apostle.

When I read the New Testament with apostolic eyes, it seems clear to me that Timothy and Titus were also vertical apostles, members of Paul's apostolic team. I now think that some biblical scholar in times past made an unfortunate mistake by nicknaming Paul's epistles to Timothy and Titus pastoral epistles. It would have been more accurate, in my opinion, to call them apostolic epistles.

For instance, Paul sends Timothy to Philippi, not to serve as pastor but to minister to the Philippians apostolically on behalf of Paul (see Phil. 2:19-29). Then he says he is also sending Epaphroditus to them as a "messenger," which is a translation of the Greek *apóstolon*, or apostle. Clearly, then, both Timothy and Epaphroditus were apostles, and more specifically, vertical apostles.

Another example could be Paul's writing to Titus: "For this reason I left you in Crete, that you should set in order the things that are lacking, and appoint elders in every city as I commanded you" (Titus 1:5). This is an apostolic word for two main reasons:

1. The phrase "set in order" exactly describes one of the central roles of an apostle. Because of the spiritual gift that God has given to apostles, they receive divine assistance in bringing order to what God is trying to do with His people. Do you want to know how to set a certain situation in order? Ask an apostle!

2. Paul told Titus to "appoint elders." In New Testament terms, elders is another word for the pastors of the churches. At that time, all churches were house churches, and each one was governed by an elder. Pastors did not appoint elders back then, apostles appointed elders.

Later on in the same chapter, Paul uses these rather startling words to warn Titus about the people to whom Paul is sending him: "One of them, a prophet of their own, said, 'Cretans are always liars, evil beasts, lazy gluttons.' This testimony is true. Therefore rebuke them sharply, that they may be sound in the faith" (Titus 1:12,13). This, obviously, is not typical pastoral language! Most pastors try to be much more politically correct, carefully measuring their words so as not to offend anyone unnecessarily. I must admit that not all apostles whom I know are quite as abrupt as Paul, but some are. Paul's epistle to Titus, then, appears to be more of an *apostolic* epistle than a *pastoral* epistle. It is one vertical apostle sending some advice to another vertical apostle.

2. HORIZONTAL APOSTLES

A major reason I was so elated when Roger Mitchell introduced me to the term "horizontal apostle" is because this is the category into which I personally fit. As I will explain in more detail in another chapter, I knew for some time that God had given me the gift of apostle, but I would never discuss it in public because I did not know what kind of apostle I was. I knew I *was not* a vertical apostle like almost all other apostles I had met up to that time, but I could not affirm what I *was* until I had the vocabulary to express it. So I kept quiet.

Unlike vertical apostles, horizontal apostles do have authority over other apostles, either for a defined, prolonged period of time or, in other cases, for a season or a particular assignment. Their sphere of authority is broader (though not necessarily greater or stronger) and, thus, horizontal.

How does a horizontal apostle operate?

The best way I can answer that question is to point to a biblical example of a horizontal apostle, namely James of Jerusalem. James is the one who convened the famous Council of Jerusalem, recorded in Acts 15. He was the brother of Jesus, the son of Mary and Joseph of Nazareth. This James was not one of the original 12 apostles. There were two apostles named James among the original 12. One, James the son of Alphaeus, we know very few details about. The other was James the son of Zebedee, who was the brother of John and a member of Jesus' inner circle: Peter, James and John. He was executed by King Herod, as recorded in Acts 12, so he was not alive at the time the other James, the brother of Jesus, called together the Council of Jerusalem.

A Major Problem in the Church

Just to refresh our memories, a major problem had arisen in the Church. All the first believers in Jesus were Jews who practiced circumcision and kept the law of Moses. True, a large number of Samaritans had been converted, but they also practiced circumcision. The problem began when Peter went to the house of Cornelius, the Roman centurion, and some uncircumcised Gentiles were saved. The problem was further compounded when Gentile house churches were planted in Antioch and when Paul and Barnabas embarked on their mission specifically to the Gentiles. Some Messianic Jews in Jerusalem even sent their own kind of missionaries on the trail of Paul and Barnabas to tell

Paul's Gentile converts they had to be circumcised if they wanted to be considered true believers in Christ (see Acts 15:1).

This was the kind of situation that could not be swept under
the rug. As a matter of fact, in retrospect we see that this problem revolved around one of the most challenging issues all cross-
cultural missionaries face: the process of contextualizing the
gospel in different cultures. If the matter had not been resolved
back then, in all probability the Church would have died out
when Jerusalem was later destroyed by the Romans in A.D. 70.
That obviously was not God's will, so how was the problem han-
dled?

James did what a good horizontal apostle should do in a situation like that, he called all the vertical apostles together, along
with the elders, presumably the elders of the house churches
there in Jerusalem. The Bible says, "Now the apostles and elders
came together to consider this matter" (Acts 15:6).

An Apostolic Dream Team

Just think about the people who were probably sitting together
in that room when the Council of Jerusalem began. Over here
was John. Over there was Peter. Then there were Bartholomew
and Thomas and Andrew and Thaddaeus and Peter and Philip,
just to mention some from the original 12. But Paul and
Barnabas were also present. Possibly Matthias was there, as well as
Andronicus and Titus and Junia and Apollos and Epaphroditus,
and who knows how many others. This was an all-star lineup, an
apostolic dream team!

As I look down that list of superstars, a radical thought
comes to mind. It could well be that no single one of them could
have successfully called the Council of Jerusalem. Why do I say
this? I will admit that things might have been different then, but

I do know that today it is quite difficult for a vertical apostle to call together other peer-level vertical apostles and see them respond. Vertical apostles often do not get along very well on a level deeper than mere cordiality.

For a first-century example, take Peter and Paul. From all appearances, they did not like each other too much. In fact, each one criticized the other right in the Bible! Paul wrote that "when Peter had come to Antioch, I withstood him to his face, because he was to be blamed" (Gal. 2:11). Then later, Peter said that Paul's epistles were so hard to understand that some "[twisted them] to their own destruction" (see 2 Pet. 3:16). While I have no way of knowing for sure, it could well have been that if Peter had called the meeting Paul would not have come or vice versa.

But James was the one who called the meeting. This is one of the things that horizontal apostles can usually do better than vertical apostles. I have noticed that when vertical apostles attempt to gather peers together, questions of a possible hidden agenda often begin to surface in the minds of some. Such distrust is usually not articulated, but nevertheless it frequently influences decisions relating to whether certain individuals should or should not attend a given gathering (such as the Council of Jerusalem). On the other hand, horizontal apostles have been positioned by God so that they usually do not appear quite as threatening.

James Takes Charge

How did James run the meeting? Very simply, he let everyone talk. In Luke's report in Acts 15, he quotes some Pharisees, he quotes Peter, and he quotes Barnabas and Paul. Obviously, this is not a transcript of the entire proceedings. If it were, the Council would have dismissed at the first coffee break.

Presumably everyone there would have been given the opportunity to say everything they wanted to say, and typically apostles are not at a loss for words. Luke does not tell us how many days the Council lasted. But he does imply that everyone had said his peace, because he writes, "And after they had become silent" (Acts 15:13).

Now it was James's turn. Here is where apostolic authority really kicked in. Keep in mind that when I described apostolic authority in the last chapter, I said that this authority only works in a given apostle's sphere. The very fact that all the others showed up at James's invitation was proof enough that this was James's sphere of authority. There was no doubt in James's mind or in the minds of the other apostles present that, for this particular occasion, divine authority had been delegated to this horizontal apostle.

That is why James could say, "Men and brethren, listen to *me*" (Acts 15:13, emphasis mine). James did not say, "There are obviously two different but very legitimate opinions here, and we must respect the sincerity of all parties. Would you agree we form a study commission and that they bring back a report in six months?" Nor did he even say, "I will now entertain a motion to resolve the issue and we will vote on it." I mention these options because these are the ways we deal with many issues in our churches and denominations today. But that is not the way apostolic leadership operates. James did not take a democratic approach. He said, "Listen to *me*."

"Therefore I Judge"

After summarizing the significant parts of the arguments he had heard, James then says, "Therefore *I judge*" (Acts 15:19, emphasis mine). I have italicized this so we see clearly the practical biblical application of what I said in the last chapter, namely that the most radical difference between traditional churches and new apostolic churches is the amount of spiritual authority delegated by the Holy Spirit to *individuals*. James used the first person singular, "I."

This has proven to be a proper and anointed use of apostolic authority, because James's verdict has held up through two millennia of the expansion of the Christian movement: "We should not trouble those from among the Gentiles who are turning to God" (Acts 15:19). I elaborate on this in detail in my commentary on Acts, where I say without hesitation: "James's conclusion constitutes the most important missiological statement ever made this side of Pentecost."[3]

What was the reaction of the participants? Did they accuse James of being a dictator? Did they feel that their rights had been violated? Did a protest group emerge from those who might have disagreed? None of the above. Rather, "It pleased the apostles and elders, with the whole church" (Acts 15:22); and "It seemed good to the Holy Spirit, and to us" (Acts 15:28). They understood and accepted apostolic leadership, in this case from a horizontal apostle.

The Apostolic Council for Educational Accountability
As a personal example, in recent years it seems that God has given me a horizontal apostolic ministry. I believe that I have responsibility for some horizontal spheres of authority such as apostles, prophets, prayer leaders and educators. For example, in June 1998 I called together the educators affiliated with the various apostolic networks that I was in touch with across the country, and around 100 of them showed up. They represented some 45 base institutions such as Bible institutes, leadership

training schools and ministry schools. Counting their branch institutions around the world, over 1,000 schools were represented.

In order to allow as many of them as possible to speak over the two days of meetings, I arranged the program by panels comprised of four individuals each. On the second day, one of the panels addressed the issues related to accreditation. Because I had been teaching in an accredited graduate school, Fuller Theological Seminary, I expected the members of the panel to agree that accreditation was necessary. They then would have discussed the pros and cons of existing accrediting associations. Instead, much to my surprise, all the panel members looked at accreditation as a dead-end street that, for the most part, could actually *prevent* some institutions from being all that God wanted them to be.

I introduced the next panel, but to be honest, I was in such a state of shock over accreditation that I could not pay much attention to what the panel was talking about. The next thing I knew, I had my yellow pad out and I was receiving revelation from God as to what He wanted us to do about traditional accreditation. I stepped outside, checked a couple of things with my staff and then asked the leader of the current panel to finish 15 minutes early because I had an announcement to make. He did, and I announced that we were going to establish a creative alternative to accreditation, the Apostolic Council for Educational Accountability (ACEA). I outlined how we would all become members of ACEA and how we would hold each other accountable for excellence. We would not be governed by some relatively abstract accrediting manual, but by God's purpose for each one of our institutions.

As in the Council of Jerusalem, this decision was not determined by study committees or by Roberts' Rules of Order.

Within an hour after I received the revelation, I made the announcement and the people there were saying words to the effect, "It seems good to the Holy Spirit and to us."

Traditional church leaders might look upon this process as autocratic or dictatorial or arrogant on my part. I understand this because I have operated out of the traditional mold for most of my ministry. But now I also understand apostolic leadership. The formation of the ACEA, which many institutions have come to regard as a blessing of God for which they have been waiting for years, is just one example of how apostolic leadership—in this case horizontal apostolic leadership—is supposed to operate.

3. HYPHENATED APOSTLES

Many apostles are not just apostles. Some have other gifts and offices as well. I call these individuals hyphenated apostles. I first got this idea from Bill Hamon who writes about "apostolic-apostles," "prophetic-apostles," "evangelistic-apostles," "pastoral-apostles" and "teacher-apostles."[4]

For example, when Paul wrote to Timothy, at one point he described himself by saying: "I was appointed a preacher, an apostle, and a teacher of the Gentiles" (2 Tim. 1:11). He could presumably be seen, then, as a preacher-apostle-teacher. I do not mean that this would constitute an exhaustive list of Paul's ministries, because it does appear to be little more than an off-the-cuff remark.

Or take Timothy himself as another example. I believe I could make a case for describing Timothy as an apostle-evangelist or possibly an evangelist-apostle. Why do I say this? I have already given my reasons for concluding that Timothy was an apostle, a member of Paul's apostolic team. But I think he was also an evangelist, because Paul said to him, "Do the work of an evangelist, fulfill your ministry" (2 Tim. 4:5). Presumably, Timothy's *ministry* was that of an evangelist, and I would assume he was recognized as having the office of evangelist as mentioned in the list from Ephesians 4:11 (emphasis mine): "apostles," "prophets," "*evangelists,*" " pastors" and "teachers."

The subject of hyphenated apostles is a relatively recent point of discussion among leaders of the New Apostolic Reformation, and some of us are still trying to get used to describing ourselves in these categories. For example, Bill Hamon sees himself as a prophet-apostle (not, by the way, an apostle-prophet). I would describe myself as a teacher-apostle. No one has ever confused me with a prophet, evangelist or pastor. I would think that John Kelly of the International Coalition of Apostles is an unhyphenated apostle. By this I do not mean that John does not prophesy or teach or evangelize or extend pastoral care, but I do mean that none of these would constitute an *office* on the level of the office of apostle that he has held for some time.

It is also quite possible that a given apostle can be hyphenated as both vertical and horizontal. Lawrence Khong of Faith Community Baptist Church in Singapore, for example, serves as a vertical apostle in his own FCBC international apostolic network, but when he goes to Taiwan he ministers to churches across the board as a very influential horizontal apostle.

In my book *Apostles of the City*, I develop this next thought in more detail, but meanwhile let me just mention it here in passing. I have a hypothesis that pastors of dynamic, growing churches of more than 700 to 800 members should, for the most part, be regarded as having the offices of pastor-apostle, or in some cases apostle-pastor. This will become an extremely important concept when we begin attempting to discern territorial apostolic leadership for transforming our cities.

4. Marketplace Apostles

The three kinds of apostles I have described, vertical apostles, horizontal apostles and hyphenated apostles, minister mostly within the boundaries of the Church. Marketplace apostles minister mostly *outside* the Church, although all of them need to be rooted in and covered by a local church in order to minister effectively.

The existence of marketplace apostles is based on an assumption. I feel quite strongly that God does not desire His kingdom be limited to the existing Church. Granted, the Church is and will continue to be an essential part of the kingdom of God. But I believe that God wants to move His kingdom through the warp and woof of society in general. Our prayer, "Your will be done on earth as it is in heaven" (Matt. 6:11), is proof enough of this assumption. The transformation of society for Christ, and nothing less, must be our goal.

How will this be done?

Quite obviously, God will do this through His people. In the United States, and in many other nations as well, the people of God are already scattered throughout most levels of society. We gather together with fellow Christians one, two or three times a week, but the rest of our time is spent out there in the marketplace. We realize that God has placed us out there in the world to be salt and light to those around us, but we live with a pervasive sense of frustration because we are not seeing the changes in the spiritual climate that we have desired. Why does it seem that God has not answered our prayers for societal change?

I believe the answer to this question goes back to the main premise of this book, namely that apostles and prophets are the foundation of the Church. The people of God are out there in force, but the critical mass for change has not been reached because the spiritual government is not yet in place. Individuals are doing what they can, but their best efforts are scattered in numerous directions, and therefore they do not make the desired impact on their surroundings.

It is more than likely that God has already placed true apostles throughout the marketplace. They have not been that effective in their ministries, however, because they have not been recognized for what they are. First, they have not recognized themselves as apostles, in many cases because the thought has never entered their minds.

Second, marketplace apostles have not as yet been acknowledged and affirmed as apostles by the other believers already out there day after day. When this scenario changes, and I sense it will be changing very soon, the kingdom of God will be in a position to bring explosive transforming power to all levels of society.

I believe there are apostles of finance, technology, medicine, industry, education, the military, government, law, communications, business, transportation, nuclear science, agriculture and a hundred other segments of society. When these marketplace apostles begin to move into their rightful place under the powerful anointing of God—watch out! Revival will be right around the corner!

I will be surprised if the ministry of marketplace apostles does not become one of the hot topics of the next few years. I believe in it so strongly that I have been bold enough to include Marketplace Ministries as one of the elective concentrations in my new school, Wagner Leadership Institute. Rich Marshall, a true pioneer in this area, is the concentration coordinator.

We have examined the premise that while all apostles have the same spiritual gift, not all of them look or act exactly the same. Understanding this will clear the way for the divinely ordered government of the Church to come into its rightful place. Vertical apostles, horizontal apostles, hyphenated apostles and marketplace apostles all have crucial roles to play in the advancement of the kingdom of God in our days.

Notes
1. C. Peter Wagner, *Your Spiritual Gifts Can Help Your Church Grow*, rev. ed. (Ventura, CA: Regal Books, 1994), p. 231.
2. C. Peter Wagner, *Churchquake!* (Ventura, CA: Regal Books, 1999), p. 108.
3. C. Peter Wagner, *Lighting the World* (Ventura, CA: Regal Books, 1995), p. 242.
4. Dr. Bill Hamon, *Apostles, Prophets and the Coming Moves of God* (Shippensburg, PA: Destiny Image, 1997), p. 227.

Chapter Four

WHAT APOSTLES NEED

As we have seen, apostles have a great deal of gifts and talents. They have authority, character, gifting, humility, spheres, followers, vision, and they receive revelation. This is all well and good, and it should be a great cause of rejoicing and encouragement to all of us.

But apostles are not perfect; not by any means. We still have a long way to go to get it all together so that God can do all He wants to do in these coming days.

As I see it, there are at least five areas in which most of today's apostles need considerable improvement. By saying this, I am not putting down apostolic leadership in the slightest. After all, this is such a new area of ministry for most of us that we are still trying our best to learn the rules of the game. It takes time. In a few years, things will probably be different. But if the New Apostolic Reformation is to advance, there is no better time to start making the improvements than now.

1. Apostles Need Positive Relationships with Prophets

Since apostles and prophets together form the foundation of the Church, one would think they would typically get along well with each other. But such is not always the case. This is so important that I have dedicated an entire chapter to it later on (see chapter 6). But meanwhile, I do not feel I can make a list of the main things apostles still need without including this item, and I have chosen to place it first because I believe it is so crucial.

I mentioned earlier that apostles receive revelation in two different ways. The source of the revelation in both cases is God Himself. Sometimes God chooses to give the revelation to apostles directly, but at other times He gives the revelation through prophets. Amos 3:7 says, "Surely the Lord GOD does nothing, unless He reveals His secret to His servants the prophets."

I was not always aware of this as God's Plan A, so to speak. Clearly, God is not *limited* to revealing Himself through prophets, but it may well be His preferred way. I believe in this so much that I have come to depend greatly on what God says to me through prophets and intercessors. A good number of my personal intercessors have the gift of prophecy, so when they speak I listen carefully. Since 1989 Doris and I have kept what we call the *Wagner Prophetic Journal*. It is a three-ring notebook in which we enter the prophecies we consider important. We now have accumulated over 100 typewritten pages of prophecies, single spaced.

I will quote from the *Prophetic Journal* from time to time in these chapters for the purpose of illustrating personally how apostles and prophets can relate positively to each other. As I look back at the prophecies we have received over recent years, I must say that every time God has moved us to a new level of ministry, He revealed it first through his servants the prophets.

At this point in my life, the major prophetic voice for me is Chuck Pierce, who also serves as our I-1 intercessor, but others also speak into our lives on a fairly regular basis. (The *I* stands for our personal intercessors, while the number designation—1, 2 or 3—refers to the level of intercession provided, 1 being the highest, most involved level. For more about personal intercessors, see my book *Prayer Shield*).

2. APOSTLES NEED PERSONAL INTERCESSORS

Here is a very important axiom: the higher individuals move in Christian leadership, the higher they move on Satan's hit list. Spiritual warfare becomes more and more intense for them, and therefore, increased protection is absolutely necessary. Every leader is personally responsible for putting on the full armor of God that we read about in Ephesians 6, including the shield of faith. But it does not follow from this that such individual protection will suffice in every case. It is a necessary starting point, but there is more. God has also given the spiritual gift of intercession to many members of the Body of Christ, and some intercessors have received specific calls or assignments to stand in the gap for Christian leaders.

I wrote my 1992 book, *Prayer Shield*, in order to help connect pastors to the intercessors who should be praying for them. I believed then, and I believe now, that this is the most important book I have ever written for pastors. Since then I have heard numerous testimonies from leaders whose lives, families and ministries reached new levels as soon as they began to receive prayer from personal intercessors. Personal intercession and prayer covering is not only a good theory, but it also is one of those theories that definitely works!

In *Prayer Shield* the word "apostles" does not appear because when I wrote the book, apostles had not yet appeared on my mental radar screen. If I were to write the book today, however, it should go without saying that I would stress strongly the absolute need for apostles to enlist intercessors as their personal prayer shields. It might well be that of all Christian leaders, apostles need intercession more than any other group.

Having said this, I must record my surprise when I discovered that not just one, but many recognized apostles have not yet taken the need for personal intercession very seriously. I hope this state of affairs changes rapidly, and I am confident that it will. Actually, I am finding that some apostles have never really thought of recruiting intercessors, but as soon as they hear about it they begin to do it.

Two of the most prominent apostles of the New Testament, Paul and Peter, are leaders who serve as examples of the positive ministry of intercessors.

In writing to the Philippians, Paul mentions two women there, Euodia and Syntyche, who in all probability served Paul as personal intercessors. Paul speaks of them as "these women who labored with me in the gospel" (Phil. 4:3). A more literal translation of the text would be "these women who did spiritual warfare on my behalf." My wife, Doris, and I have 22 personal intercessors who continually do spiritual warfare on our behalf, and we are convinced that without them the enemy would have taken us out of the picture long ago. They are the most important group of people in our lives with the exception of our immediate family.

At one point, the enemy tried hard to take Peter out of the picture, using King Herod as his chief instrument. Herod had two Christian leaders on his hit list at the time: James and Peter.

He succeeded in killing James, but he could not kill Peter. Why? "Peter was therefore kept in prison, but constant prayer was offered to God for him by the church" (Acts 12:5). Later on, we get the detail that the prayer meeting for Peter was held in the house of Mary, the mother of Mark (see Acts 12:12). It could well be, therefore, that Mary served as what I would call Peter's I-1 intercessor. Powerful prayer can save lives!

3. Apostles Need Recognition and Affirmation

The apostolic movement cannot flourish if no one knows about it. It is true that there are some who oppose the contemporary use of the title "apostle." But to succumb to this opposition and decide to avoid mentioning apostles as such is a self-defeating decision. I believe that the time has come to be much more direct and forthright than we have sometimes been about making the apostolic movement public.

Recognition and affirmation must begin with apostles themselves. I know by personal experience that it is not an easy thing to cross the line and start referring to oneself as an apostle. I go into detail on this important matter later in the next chapter. Of the 18 apostles I invited to do first-person chapters in my book *The New Apostolic Churches,* only 2 of the 18 allowed me to use "apostle" as their title: Apostle John Kelly and Apostle John Eckhardt. The other 16 apostles preferred me to use other titles, such as "president" or "pastor" or "bishop" or "director" or "founder" or "superintendent."

Interestingly, each and every one agreed that they were apostles. But when I cross-examined them as to why they did not want me to use the title, the most frequent response were words to the effect that using "apostle" might precipitate battles they did not particularly want to fight at this point in time. Most of them stressed that the important thing was the *function* of an apostle, not the *title* per se.

I am not sure I agree that the use of the title "apostle" should be considered optional in this day and age. The most remarkable phenomenon in Church life that we have seen in generations is taking place right now, and the government of the Church is at the heart of these changes. Apostles and prophets are now being recognized as the foundation of the Church as the Bible says they should be. Let us overcome our inhibitions and take our lead from role models such as Paul and Peter who begin epistles with "Paul, an apostle of Jesus Christ" or "Peter, an apostle of Jesus Christ."

Although the recognition and affirmation of apostles must begin with the apostles themselves, if the movement is going to gain and sustain its vitality, the rest of the Body of Christ—and then the public in general—must recognize apostles as well.

As I mentioned in chapter 1, the Church has become quite comfortable using titles for evangelists (Evangelist Billy Graham), pastors (Pastor or Reverend Robert Schuller) and teachers (Doctor or Professor Peter Wagner). Therefore, the idea of using titles for the offices of Ephesians 4:11 has not been rejected in principle.

Granted, it would not be realistic to expect a knee-jerk reaction on the part of the Christian public when it comes to acknowledging the reemergence of an office in the Church. It may come as a surprise to some to learn that the office of pastor, as we know it, only emerged after the Protestant Reformation. That means that in the 2000-year history of the Church, the commonly defined role of pastor has only been recognized for 1/5 of that time (i.e., 400-plus years). Even more, the office of evangelist was not recognized by the Church in general until the time of Charles Finney, only 150 years ago. In fact, there was much debate in the mid-1800s among Christian leaders as to whether it was proper to recognize an individual as an evangelist. Some theologians condemned Finney as an advocate of what they derisively called "new measures."

We should not be surprised, therefore, if some choose to argue against the contemporary office of apostle. I have actually seen this labeled as heresy, in print. But, while I am not an advocate of direct polemics, I do feel that we who believe we are hearing what the Spirit is saying to the churches these days should not be passive. One of the ways to be positively aggressive is to start using the title "apostle" more than we have been. We should continue to use "apostolic" as an adjective. We can even try to make this into a noun and talk about "the apostolic." But we should also recognize and affirm "Apostle So-and-So" whenever the opportunity arises.

4. APOSTLES NEED OPEN COMMUNICATION CHANNELS

Apostolic ministries rise or fall on personal relationships. And relationships are built and sustained on communication. Therefore, apostles must give a very high priority to keeping communication channels open.

There are two levels on which communication is most vital: (1) communication with followers and (2) communication with apostolic peers. Let us look at them.

Communication with Followers

Most apostles whom I know communicate well with their followers. That is a major reason why their apostolic networks remain intact. Apostles are frequent flyers. I will not forget seeing the home that Bill Hamon custom designed and built. The closet he and his wife, Evelyn, use is not just a walk-in, but a room in itself. Their clothes hang around the walls, but the centerpiece is a 10 x 5-foot island upon which they can pack their open suitcases with as little effort as possible. The room is even equipped with an ironing board. The Hamons' lifestyle is one of traveling far and wide to be with the leaders in their Christian International Network.

Apostolic communication is as personal as possible. Printed materials like newsletters are not as common as they are in traditional denominations because they are seen as rather impersonal. Many apostles love to use the telephone. In fact, it is almost impossible to get some of the apostles whom I know to write an old-fashioned letter. To communicate with them one had better know their personal assistant on a first-name basis in order to tie down a telephone appointment.

A very prominent form of communication with followers is through conferences. Usually these are regularly scheduled at determined times of the year. Members of an apostolic network will gladly budget considerable sums of money in order to attend these conferences. That is where they make firsthand contact with the apostle and get to build the all-important personal relationships.

Communication with Peers

As the New Apostolic Reformation has been emerging, the opportunities for apostles to build personal relationships with one another have been limited. Vertical apostles consider their primary responsibility to minister within their particular apostolic network. They understand their spheres of authority and that is where they feel the most comfortable. In some cases, this ministry requires such an incredible output of energy that very little time can be allotted to keeping up with other apostolic networks, to say nothing about apostles attempting to build personal relationships with other apostles.

This is an area where horizontal apostles have a special ability to convene other apostles (e.g., vertical), as we have already examined in the case of James at the Council of Jerusalem.

The National Symposium on the Post-Denominational Church

Back in 1996, just as I was in the process of trying to understand the New Apostolic Reformation, I called together the National Symposium on the Post-Denominational Church, which took place at Fuller Seminary. Around 500 leaders attended, and I was able to get almost 50 of them onto the platform to address the gathering. Bill Hamon says the meeting "was a historical occasion in God's annals of Church history. It was prophetically orchestrated by the Holy Spirit to fulfill God's progressive purpose of bringing His Church to its ultimate destiny."[1] At that time I did not even know the terms "New Apostolic Reformation" or "horizontal apostles," but I now realize it was only the anointing of God on me as a horizontal apostle that enabled me to call such a meeting.

Why did Bill Hamon consider this meeting historic? He says it was one of the first major opportunities that apostles had to build meaningful personal relationships with peer-level apostles from networks with which they previously had had little contact.

A follow-up to that meeting was the International Apostolic Team Summit in Colorado Springs in 1999, which we convened. Almost 3,000 people showed up for the event, which was another tangible expression of the desire of apostolic leaders to be exposed to the wider circle of the New Apostolic Reformation and to free-flowing communication channels.

The International Coalition of Apostles

As I am writing this, a new organization is springing up, designed to help meet the needs of apostles for ongoing peer-level communication with one another. It is called the International Coalition of Apostles (ICA). I am aware of the risk of mentioning a fledgling organization in a book like this, but I have chosen to take the risk because I feel so strongly that this will be a winner in the days to come.

After serving for many years as a vertical apostle over Antioch Churches and Ministries (ACM), John Kelly, the coauthor of *End Time Warriors*, began to sense that the Lord was moving him from being a vertical apostle to a horizontal apostle. In 1999 he turned the reins of ACM over to his disciple, Apostle Gary Kivelowitz, in order to free himself to give leadership to ICA. In his travels to many parts of the world, Kelly learned that apostles were wanting to be a part of some kind of structure that would facilitate peer-level apostolic communication. As he prayed about this, Kelly felt that God wanted him to initiate a career change and help give birth to the International Coalition of Apostles.

John Kelly then set up an apostolic council to which he would be accountable throughout the formation and execution of ICA. I was invited to be a member of the council, and I have now agreed to serve as presiding apostle. I am very excited about my role of leading ICA and about the organization's tremendous potential to raise communication among apostles to a new level worldwide. It will help a great deal in meeting the need for viable communication channels in the New Apostolic Reformation.

5. APOSTLES NEED FUNCTIONAL ACCOUNTABILITY

Local church pastors who belong to apostolic networks understand that they are accountable to their apostles. But to whom are the apostles accountable? Through the years of my association with some of the top leaders of the New Apostolic Reformation, I have frequently raised this question. The answers, to be truthful, have not always satisfied me. It is clear that almost all apostles sincerely recognize their need for functional accountability. Many of them, however, say that they are "working on it," meaning they themselves are not satisfied with the status quo either. They know that there must be a better way.

This is not to say that accountability systems already in place in the New Apostolic Reformation are all nonfunctional. It could appear that a head apostle who appoints an apostolic council to help administer his network could not really be accountable to that council of subordinates. This may be the case in some networks, but in at least one of them, Antioch Churches and Ministries, it did prove to be functional when crunch time came.

Antioch Churches and Ministries
A test case arose in ACM when John Kelly decided to pass the baton of apostolic leadership from the first-generation apostle

to the second-generation apostle, Gary Kivelowitz, in 1999. To date, we do not have many examples of this kind of transfer of the mantle of apostolic authority. In other similar situations, the network tended to dissolve when the founding apostle left, and in some cases the apostolic network routinized (i.e., lost its original vision and regressed into an administrative, rather than leader-driven, form of government) and became a denomination. In ACM, neither of these steps backward seems to be on the horizon. A good lesson from the ACM case is that founding apostles like John Kelly do well to make sure their successors are properly identified and trained.

Unexpectedly, when Gary Kivelowitz took over the leadership of ACM and when all information was made available, he found in them some things he felt were out of order. They did not involve anything like immorality or criminal action, but there were some decisions made in the context of Kelly's management style that Gary and the apostolic council felt were unwise and hurtful to ACM. The apostolic council felt that these irregularities were serious enough to warrant putting Apostle Kelly under reprimand and discipline. That is why I said that the ACM situation was a test case. Would accountability really work?

Happily, it did. Covenant relationships ultimately transcended disciplinary legalism, just as they should have. Apostle Kelly responded admirably to the reprimand and discipline with humility, contrition and heartfelt repentance. The council, in turn, sincerely repented for failing to move in strongly long before this happened, back when they first suspected that John might be making some unwise decisions. In a surprisingly short period of time, mutual forgiveness was extended, all pending issues were positively resolved, and the discipline was lifted.

I tell this story, with the permission of those involved, so that all who are interested in the New Apostolic Reformation will be exposed to a real-life example of how apostolic accountability can and does function in a healthy situation. Some have suggested that one advantage denominations have over apostolic networks is they offer a more functional accountability system for their members. However, it would not be difficult to name several high-visibility leaders in denominational structures for whom established disciplinary procedures were highly ineffective. This is not to say that apostolic network accountability is flawless, because examples of failure will undoubtedly arise. But it is to say that a very high potential for integrity is not absent among contemporary apostles and in the new apostolic networks.

The New Apostolic Roundtable

In apostolic thinking, the health and well-being of a given movement will rise or fall on personal relationships. This is true within a particular apostolic network and it is also true on a broader scale among different apostolic networks. If such is the case, then it would follow that apostolic accountability must emerge from relationships.

Personal relationships can be plotted on a scale from mere acquaintance on one end to intimacy on the other end. Superficial or shallow relationships cannot be expected to spawn meaningful accountability. The deeper the relationship, then, the more authentic the potential accountability.

With these ideas in mind, I began praying some time ago about possible structures to help raise the level of relationships among apostles of different networks. I discussed this with several apostles over a period of time, and it was in a motel room in Red

Deer, Alberta, Canada, in 1999 that I believe I received the revelation to start the New Apostolic Roundtable. I discerned that it should be a small group of apostles (not more than 25) with whom I had built personal relationships. The purpose would be to establish a structure that would periodically bring the members together in a peer-level forum. Meetings would be specifically designed to enable relationships to form and blossom. Presumably, functional accountability would eventually emerge.

Part of the vision God gave me that day was that scores of such small groups of apostles would be formed in the United States and around the world. I strongly believe that this is going to happen, mostly under the leadership of horizontal apostles. In fact, I see signs of it already with groups like this being called together by my friends Ron Cottle and Stan DeKoven, two horizontal apostles here in the United States, to name two examples. Members of these groups are not "under" anyone else because all members are peers. It is important to understand that accountability among the members cannot be superimposed from the top down, but must emerge spontaneously as relationships build over time. One tool that is used to foster such accountability is the public announcement of the names involved in the group. This is not done to gain notoriety but rather to build integrity into the process.

AVOIDING THE RETURN TO DENOMINATIONALISM

Apostles need positive relationships with prophets, they need personal intercessors, they need recognition and affirmation, they need to keep communication channels open, and they need functional accountability. Let us add to this list one thing that apostles definitely do *not* need: to allow apostolic networks to revert to denominations.

I have a long section on this topic in *Churchquake!* and I believe it is one of the most important sections in the book. I do not want to repeat that material here, but I do feel that at least a reminder is necessary, knowing that not all readers of this book will have read *Churchquake!*

Broadly accepted theories of the sociology of religion hold that it is inevitable that organizations like apostolic networks (which Ernst Troeltsch and H. Richard Neibuhr would call "sects") first break off from traditional churches, but eventually they themselves become traditional churches once again. Historically, there has hardly been an exception to this rule. Max Weber would call this the routinization of charisma, and here is what almost invariably happens:

- The visionary apostolic leader starts the movement. By definition, this is a charismatic leader (not in the *theological* sense of "charisma," but rather in the *sociological* sense of the word).
- When the leader dies, the followers regroup and try to figure out how to perpetuate their leader's charisma. Usually their response is to form a rational, bureaucratic, democratic structure.
- The new leader is then selected by a *group*, so the focus of trust, and by implication the final point of authority, shifts from an individual (the apostle) to a group of persons who have the power to appoint (or remove) their leaders.

While sociologists of religion almost unanimously assume that this routinization of charisma is inevitable, I do not agree.

I think there are three components of what I like to see as a "prescription." If taken according to the doctor's orders, this prescription, in most cases, effectively prevents apostolic networks from becoming denominations.

Keep a ceiling on the number of churches in each network. One apostle, depending on several variables, can effectively oversee a network in the range of 50 to 150 churches. The formation of apostolic teams, as Sam Matthews points out in his excellent book *Apostolic Teams*, can lift the ceiling if the teams are skillfully designed and interrelated.

Constantly cultivate charisma. One of the high-priority roles of an apostle should be to raise up other apostles in the network. Many apostles cannot do this well because of resident insecurities. But if these insecurities can be overcome and if the apostle is not threatened by the emergence of those who may soon become peers, a healthy environment results.

Multiply apostolic networks. When new apostles emerge within a given apostolic network, the founding apostle should release them and bless them in every way to start their own new networks. This avoids routinization because (1) it keeps the number of churches in each network at a manageable level, and (2) it provides first-generation charismatic leadership for each new network.

If this "prescription" is implemented, the only network that is in any danger of routinization is the founding network, and in most cases, the spiritual dynamics released in the process will even prevent this from happening.

This is like parents raising their children and then releasing them to form their own new family units. The new relationship becomes an adult-to-adult relationship, but in a healthy family the respect for the parents never diminishes. Likewise, in apostolic networks the apostles over each individual network relate to each other on a peer level, but the founding apostle never ceases to be special, and in many cases, the first among equals.

As I observe the New Apostolic Reformation, I see very positive progress being made in all of the areas of both need and avoidance that I have listed. But we must not forget these prescriptive elements or expect them to happen spontaneously and without conscious effort on the part of apostolic leaders. It will take effort, but the results will be well worth it.

Note
1. Dr. Bill Hamon, *Apostles, Prophets and the Coming Moves of God* (Shippensburg, PA: Destiny Image, 1997), p. 10.

Chapter Five

BOTH APOSTLES AND PROPHETS ARE CRUCIAL

The fundamental thesis of this book is that the Church cannot be all God wants it to be unless—and until—the divinely ordained government of the Church is solidly in place. In my view, the primary governmental gifts to the Church are apostles, prophets, evangelists, pastors and teachers, according to Ephesians 4:11. In this book I have chosen to address the issues related specifically to apostles and prophets. This is not to deny the vital role of evangelists, pastors and teachers, but I have selected apostles and prophets as the focus for two reasons:

1. For many generations the Church has been comfortable with the gifts and offices of evangelist, pastor and teacher. Only in this present generation have apostles

and prophets begun to be recognized. Many church leaders still find themselves quite uncomfortable with the attempt to come to terms with the suggestion that these two offices did not cease to exist at the end of the apostolic age.

2. While all five offices have uniquely important functions to fulfill in the life and ministry of the Church, only two are specifically designated as the *foundation* of the Church, namely apostles and prophets. "The household of God [has] been built on the foundation of the apostles and prophets, Jesus Christ Himself being the chief cornerstone" (Eph. 2:19,20).

Up to this point, I have been analyzing the various aspects of the gift and office of apostle. It is time now to bring the prophets into the picture. Governmentally, apostles come first and then prophets: "And God has appointed these in the church: first apostles, second prophets" (1 Cor. 12:28). In recent times, however, prophets preceded apostles. Prophets began to be more widely recognized in the 1980s, while apostles started to come into their own only in the 1990s. This was necessary because the prophets first had to open the curtain of God's revelation to key church leaders, allowing them to look through to see that when the apostles came, it was truly something the Spirit was saying to the churches.

HOW DO APOSTLES AND PROPHETS RELATE?

I personally have a good bit more to say about apostles than about prophets because I am an apostle and I am not a prophet.

Other recent books such as Jack Deere's *Surprised by the Voice of God*, Cindy Jacobs's *The Voice of God*, Bill Hamon's *Prophets and Personal Prophecy* and Chuck Pierce's *Receiving the Word of the Lord* explain considerably more about the nature and function of prophets and prophecy than I could possibly duplicate. However, there is one crucial area that has not been dealt with in much detail in the literature, and that is how apostles and prophets specifically relate to each other in real-life ministry situations.

In his book *Apostles, Prophets and the Coming Moves of God*, Bill Hamon is one of the few who even brings this up. He includes an excellent chapter "The Special Ministries of Apostles and Prophets." It is not uncommon for other authors to describe the ministry of apostles as over and against the ministries of prophets, but Hamon is one who goes on from there to deal with their mutual relationships:

> The ethical meaning of mutualism is interdependence opposed to individualism. Mutual means that two people have so many things in common in their abilities, vision and ministries that they are interdependent on each other rather than independent of each other. There is no competitiveness [between apostles and prophets], but a complementing of each other. Their callings, ministries and destinies are linked together. They give each other their mutual respect and honor with each having acceptance and appreciation of the other.[1]

Over the relatively few years of my personal apostolic ministry, I am fortunate to have been closely associated with some of the most respected prophets of the day. In this area, therefore, I can go beyond theory and am able to base some of my conclusions on lessons learned the hard way—through personal experience. As I mentioned in the last chapter, one of the things that took me by surprise when I first began mixing with apostles and prophets was that they did not always seem to get along well with each other.

Bill Hamon, who has the enviable advantage of being both a prophet and an apostle, warned us that this could be the case when he wrote: "Some prophets are getting nervous and concerned about the restoration of apostles and are fearful that they will try to structure them into a restricted realm that God never intended."[2]

DISCOVERING THAT ONE IS AN APOSTLE

In this day and age it is not that easy for leaders to come to the conclusion that they might be authentic apostles. For example, John Kelly, whose apostolic office few would question, writes, "I believe I functioned in an apostolic role for a minimum of 10 years before I could say I was an apostle. It was not a goal of mine to operate as an apostle; it just happened. Only sons can promote a father, and as I functioned in the ministry, this is the title they gave me."[3] Most of the apostles with whom I associate most closely have similar testimonies.

It was only in 1993 that I began taking seriously the notion that there actually were contemporary apostles. I had not doubted it in theory before 1993, but it was then that I began to understand how the theory was being lived out in practice. From that point on, I underwent a rapid paradigm shift. I want to explain this shift with a special emphasis on the role that prophets played in my personal journey.

KEEPING A PROPHETIC JOURNAL

As I mentioned before, my wife, Doris, and I keep the *Prophetic Journal* in which we record prophecies that we judge to be significant for our own lives and ministry. Because of a certain level of visibility that we either enjoy or endure, depending on the day, we probably receive more direct personal prophecies than many others. The procedure we have chosen is to filter out and preserve only those prophetic words that we judge to be, let us say, 9 or 10 on a scale of potential personal relevance. Admittedly, this is a very subjective procedure.

Doris and I would like to think we have the perfect mind of the Holy Spirit in every one of these decisions, but we are realistic enough to doubt very much if such is the case. Our own emotions and desires undoubtedly play some part in this, but we try to keep them to a minimum. I do not have the exact figure, but I know that we preserve a very small percentage of the total number of prophetic words we receive.

The reason we keep our *Prophetic Journal* is because we believe God does, indeed, speak through His prophets today, and some of the things He speaks are meant specifically for us. One of the functions of prophecy, as I understand it, is to clue us in to some of the things we should be praying about. Another is to prepare us or give us a heads up about what God has in mind for our lives and ministries. Some prophecies give us the encouragement we need to take that next step which may seem at the moment like a difficult thing to do.

If Doris and I did not have our *Prophetic Journal*, I do not know how we could accurately keep track of the ways that our lives have been so strongly influenced by prophecy. Some people might have such sharp memories that they can remember the details of prophecies, but that is not true for us. In many situations, it is only after the fact that we go back and discover, much to our amazement, how God has divinely ordained us to be where we are now.

The First Prophecy

We began recording prophecies in June 1989, and the first was given to me by Joy Dawson in the home of Ben Jennings of Campus Crusade. We were preparing for the on-site intercession that would take place during the Lausanne II Congress in Manila. Joy first prayed that I would receive an impartation of the fear of the Lord at an entirely new level in my life. She then said:

> *The fear of the Lord is the only thing that will release you from the fear of man. God is going to raise up in you a deep hatred of evil and He is going to open up doors of increased authority in the Body of Christ in the days to come, despite the opposition that will arise.*

At this writing, we have now entered 103 additional single-spaced, typewritten pages into this three-ring binder.

How do these prophecies relate to my current understanding that God has given me the office of apostle?

As I have tried to trace this back, it could be said that Joy Dawson's prophecy of *increased authority in the Body of Christ* would clearly apply. At that point, in 1989, I knew virtually nothing about apostles, apostolic ministry or apostolic authority. But, looking back, there it is!

The first time I heard the word "apostle" used for me in prophecy was in July 1995 at a Voice of God conference in Colorado Springs. At that time, Cindy Jacobs had a prophetic word for Doris and me. Before I go into detail, let me say that the majority of prophetic words we choose to enter into the *Prophetic*

Journal come from our personal intercessors, many of whom also have the gift of prophecy. There is a certain touch of authenticity that personal prophecy carries when it flows from serious, ongoing intercession for a given leader. Doris and I have come to recognize that through the years.

Cindy Jacobs is one of our I-2 intercessors. Here is what she prophesied:

> *The Lord would say today, "My son, Peter, today I put the anointing of apostle of prayer upon you. I put the mantle upon you of an Abraham, a patriarch, and I'm calling you forth into the land of promise. And I call you, Doris, 'Sarah'" says the Lord. "And I am calling you forth to give you many, many, many spiritual children."*

By 1995 I was coordinating the AD2000 United Prayer Track, so I knew that I had a role as a global prayer leader. But I had a difficult time with "apostle," even though Cindy presented me with a wooden staff, symbolizing authority, which I still have hanging in my study.

The Apostolic Door

Two months later, I received a prophetic word from one of our I-3 intercessors from Fort Worth, Texas, Margaret Moberly. Knowing nothing about Cindy's prophecy, she said:

> *An apostolic door has been sovereignly opened for you by the Lord Himself. Neither man nor demon will be able to shut it.*

This prophecy, however, did not cause me to jump into action and begin looking for ways it might quickly be fulfilled in my life. I did pray about it briefly, and then I all but forgot about it for more than two years.

My problem was that at this point (late 1995), I had no way to personally assimilate the knowledge God had given me, through prophets, that I had some sort of a personal apostolic role. By then I was beginning to understand what an apostle really was, and I did not doubt at all the accuracy and the validity of those prophecies. Yet, on the other hand, I could not move in the direction they indicated.

I was not exactly on hold, however, because periodically throughout those two years (1993-1995) I began recognizing deep down that I probably was an apostle of some kind. What I see as a very significant event took place in February 1998 in Dallas during a conference called Building Foundations for Revival sponsored by Global Harvest Ministries. Some say it was among the most spiritually powerful conferences we have ever done, and the presence of the Holy Spirit was definitely being felt in an extraordinary way. I was serving as master of ceremonies and trying to keep things as calm and orderly as possible.

A Spontaneous Prophetic Affirmation

Nevertheless, at one point things were not exactly calm because several spontaneous prophetic words were being given from the platform in rapid succession. I was suddenly called up front where I found myself kneeling and surrounded by several rather noisy intercessors. Jim Stevens, a recognized prophet with Bill Hamon's Christian International, took the microphone and spoke these words over me:

> *"Even from this day forward, even from this national conference, there shall be a release on your spirit. Whether you want to*

say 'apostle' or not is of no effect," says God. "The title shall rest
on you, the anointing shall rest on you, men will give it to you. It
is not something that you have sought for on your own. Men will
place it upon your back and upon your spirit, and they will draw
the apostolic from you."

During this time, I felt I was being filled with the Holy Spirit
and that I needed to take literally the word from the Lord
through Jim Stevens. So I did. If anyone asks me, I consider this
my first public recognition as an apostle.

Using the Term "Apostle"

From that time on, I definitely knew that God had given me the
gift and office of apostle, so I started using the term but only in
private conversation. The reason I could not speak it or write it
in public was because I did not yet know what kind of apostle I
was. At that point I had come to know many apostles personally, and I knew that I was not like any one of them as far as my
practical ministry was concerned. If I was going to let others
know that I was an apostle, I needed better vocabulary to communicate it.

The prophetic affirmation came in February 1998, and it
was not until seven months later that I finally received the
vocabulary I was praying for. That was when I was conversing
with Roger Mitchell of England and he first mentioned "vertical
apostles" and "horizontal apostles," as I explained in a previous
chapter. I instantly knew that I was a *horizontal* apostle. My apostolic friends, whom I knew were somehow different, turned out
to be *vertical* apostles. Now I could talk about it in public!

As it turned out, I received a formal commissioning as an
apostle by the members of the New Apostolic Roundtable,

which I described in the last chapter, on April 28, 2000. This ceremony is so new, however, that agreed-upon guidelines for making it happen are still to be determined.

PROPHETS ARE CRUCIAL

As a reminder, the Bible says that "God has appointed these in the Church: first apostles, second prophets" (1 Cor. 12:28). However, the government of the Church certainly does not end with apostles and prophets; many more offices are essential for the well-being of the Church. But just as certainly, the government of the Church does *begin* with both apostles and prophets.

I did not always think that prophets were crucial to the correct functioning of the Church. After I moved away from the cessationist theology that I had been taught in seminary, I developed a mental theological framework for accepting prophets in the contemporary Church. I had read theologian Wayne Grudem's arguments in favor of prophetic ministry and I found myself in basic agreement with him. But there were as yet no operative links between that theory and my practical day-to-day ministry. I was still not sure that there were any bona fide prophets close enough to me so that I would ever get to meet one in real life.

Wimber Persuades Wagner

The person who most helped me make the shift toward embracing prophets was John Wimber, founder of the Vineyard Movement.

Some people do not know that when John Wimber started the Anaheim Vineyard Christian Fellowship in 1977, he was my employee. In 1975 I invited John to leave his Quaker church pastorate to help me establish a church growth consultation ministry called the Charles E. Fuller Institute of Evangelism and Church Growth. Wimber soon gained the reputation as one of the premier church growth consultants in the nation, and many churches across all denominational lines were being helped.

At one point in 1977, John said, "Peter, I don't think I'm using my gift of evangelism enough in this consultation ministry. I'm just dealing with Christians day in and day out."

I replied, "I see your point. Why don't you start a new church?"

He said that he had already been thinking about it. And that—to make a long story short—was the beginning of Anaheim Vineyard. I had in mind a little Bible-study-type church where John might teach every Sunday and then come back to work for me during the week. But the rest is history. Anaheim Vineyard turned out to be one of the nation's most dynamic megachurches, and the Association of Vineyard Churches ultimately embraced 500 local churches.

Soon after that, I began teaching an adult Sunday School class, the 120 Fellowship, at Lake Avenue Congregational Church near Fuller Seminary. I taught this class of about 100 adults every Sunday for 13 years. Exciting things began happening at the Anaheim Vineyard, and almost all the class members attended Wimber's church on Sunday nights. Whenever a new emphasis came into Vineyard, within the next few months we would begin to practice it in 120 Fellowship.

The Kansas City Prophets

One of the major innovations in Vineyard came in 1989 when John Wimber linked up with Mike Bickle, Paul Cain and the Kansas City Prophets. John did not know very much about prophecy until Paul Cain called him and said the Lord had told him to go to Anaheim to visit John. Just so John would be sure that the Lord had sent Paul, there would be an earthquake under Fuller Seminary in Pasadena on the day he arrived. Sure enough, Paul Cain arrived and so did the earthquake. I spent two or three days picking up the books that had been thrown off my shelves onto my Fuller Seminary office floor in a wall-to-wall pile two to three feet deep! Cain's visit got our attention, to say the least.

Soon afterward, Wimber invited Paul to be a conference speaker in Anaheim. I was teaching a Doctor of Ministry class at the time with about 50 to 60 pastors of mostly mainline denominations, and we all decided to go hear Paul Cain on his first night at the Vineyard. Our interest in prophecy was only at the curiosity stage at best, so I must admit that there was a certain amount of skepticism throughout the group. As it turned out, it was not one of Paul Cain's better nights. When we debriefed in class the next morning, our consensus was that the notion of those with the office of prophet ministering in churches today was highly questionable.

Word of my skepticism got back to John Wimber. By now, he had bought into prophecy hook, line and sinker. So he and his wife, Carol, took Doris and me out for a nice dinner. By the end of the evening, John had thoroughly persuaded me that prophecy was for real and that I needed to tune into it. Since that day in 1989, my appreciation for prophets and my openness to receive prophetic ministry for my personal life has never stopped rising. Without that dinner, I never would have been able to write a book like this.

Practicing Prophetic Ministry

As soon as I had been convinced that prophecy was for real, I had to try it out. As I mentioned, I viewed my 120 Fellowship Sunday

School class as my spiritual experimental laboratory. It was at this time that Doris and I first met Mike and Cindy Jacobs, and I learned that Cindy had been among those recognized by some as having the office of prophet. I decided to take the 120 Fellowship class on a weekend retreat to Solvang (a nearby Danish tourist village) and invited Cindy to come and teach us about prophecy.

The retreat started very well with Cindy teaching biblical principles interlaced with many personal experiences in prophetic ministry. Early Sunday morning, however, she blindsided me. She said, "Peter, I will need a tape recorder this morning." I had no idea why she might want this because we had not planned to record the messages at this event. When I asked her, she said, "I have been teaching on prophecy for a couple of days. Today I am going to prophesy!" I was shocked! This was a Congregational church, and I knew the word would get out about what we had done. But by now I had come to trust Cindy and her integrity, so we found a tape recorder.

The prophetic ministry that day was unforgettable. I am sure today if I asked any one of those 100 or so people who were present at the retreat in Solvang, not a single one would have forgotten our sudden introduction to prophecy. Many of them had personal, life-changing experiences under the ministry of the Holy Spirit through Cindy's prophetic ministry. Many would tell you that they would not be where they are today if it were not for that retreat. Each personal prophecy was taped and we transcribed and published all of the prophecies in our class newsletter, *Body Life*, over the following few months.

A Desire to Prosper

From that time on, I took 2 Chronicles 20:20 very seriously: "Believe in the LORD your God, and you shall be established;

believe His prophets and you shall prosper." I had been established since I first believed in the Lord in 1950, but I also had a
deep desire to prosper and to be everything that God wanted me
to be. Once I started believing the prophets, prosperity in many
different senses of the word kicked in for me, my family and my
ministry, and I am at a place now that I could never have
dreamed of back in 1989.

I have been very personal in this chapter because I think this
is the best way to communicate that both apostles and prophets
are crucial if the Church is to become all that God wants it to be.
Let us now look at some more detailed analysis of how apostles
and prophets can be hitched together.

Notes
  1. Dr. Bill Hamon, *Apostles, Prophets and the Coming Moves of God* (Shippens-
     burg, PA: Destiny Image, 1997), p. 139.
  2. Ibid., p. 55.
  3. John Kelly, *End Time Warriors* (Ventura, CA: Renew, 1999), p. 106.

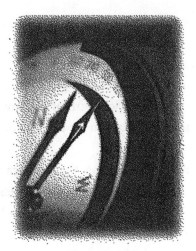

Chapter Six

HITCHING APOSTLES TO PROPHETS

I love the analogy of apostles being "hitched" to prophets like two fine draft horses are hitched to each other. Both Doris and I are dairy farmers with roots in rural upstate New York. We both lived on farms in the 1930s when draft horses were standard farm equipment. I can remember driving a team on our hay wagon when I was five years old. We had no tractor in those days.

This explains why Doris and I like to go to livestock shows where our favorite event is the draft horse competition. We love to see those magnificent Percherons and Clydesdales and Belgians and Shires working together as teams. The climax of all events is the horse pull, in which a team of two horses weighing a combined 4,500 pounds often pulls 14,000 pounds of concrete blocks on a flat sled. I remember one county fair that featured individual horse pulls. The winner pulled 5,000 pounds and the runner up pulled 4,000 pounds. But hitched together, they pulled 13,000 pounds!

What does this say about apostles and prophets? Apostles can do certain good things on their own. Prophets can do certain good things on their own. But hitched together, they can change the world! I want to explain how this can happen in real life.

PULLING TOGETHER

Many draft horse breeders take their teams from show to show on a circuit, so the same teams compete against each other more than once. It is not unusual to see one team beat another in one show and then be beaten by the other in the next show. What is the variable? The horses that pull together on a given day win. The central figure is the 180-pound teamster holding the reins and controlling more than two tons of horseflesh.

When the team is hitched to the sled, the audience becomes absolutely silent. The horses are coiled like springs, trembling and stepping around in place with pent-up nervous energy. Suddenly the teamster shouts "Giddyap!" and the horses are off! If the teamster shouts at the split second when they are both moving forward together, they win. If they are not moving in the same direction at that moment, the strongest team in the show will lose. It is as simple as that.

This is the same with apostles and prophets. Sadly, many authentic apostles and prophets are losers. They do a little, all of which may be good. But they never reach their God-given potential because they do not pull together.

On the other hand, those apostles and prophets who are winners have come to understand and appreciate their mutual roles in the kingdom of God. They know how to relate to one another in a positive way; they constantly add value to each other. As Bill Hamon would say, they are totally interdependent.

There are at least two ways, both found in the New Testament, that apostles and prophets relate to each other:

A casual relationship. Sometimes a prophet and an apostle will find themselves meeting together at a given time, and the prophet might have a word from God to give to the apostle. This has happened to me frequently. In the New Testament, the encounter Paul had with Agabus illustrates this point (see Acts 21:10-13). I like to refer to this as a Paul-Agabus relationship. Paul and Agabus did not have an ongoing relationship, simply a casual one.

A structured relationship. In this case the apostle and the prophet have placed themselves in a position to communicate with each other on a regular, ongoing basis. The relationship can be so close that their normal modus operandi is never to enter into important ministry activity without the participation of or at least the knowledge of the other. The apostle Paul, who brought the prophet Silas into his core ministry team, models this for us (see Acts 15:40). This Paul-Silas relationship would see the two as being "harnessed" together, while the Paul-Agabus relationship would see them as being "tied" together.

My apostolic relationship with prophet Chuck Pierce is a current example of a Paul-Silas relationship. We are harnessed together since we are both officers of Global Harvest Ministries. We live in the same city, we work in the same facility, and we frequently travel together and minister at the same events. However, we also take pains to be sure that neither one of us *controls* the other. I am not trying to make Chuck over into my image, and he is not trying to make me over into his image. The fact that we are vastly different from each other in background, temperament, age and giftings serves to strengthen the relationship. We have entered into a working covenant based on mutual respect and trust. Neither of us is intimidated or awed by the other, which allows a mutual openness and vulnerability. The net result is that we continually add value to each other and to each other's ministry.

TRANSITIONING THE GLOBAL PRAYER MOVEMENT

In chapter 2, I told the story of when Chuck Pierce gave me the prophetic word about how I needed to receive the Lord's vision for where the global prayer movement was to go after our decade of praying for the 10/40 Window. This was one of the most far-reaching decisions I have been called upon to make. It needed to be done quickly, and it had to be my decision. It was one of those things that an apostle cannot delegate. I was amazed that once I asked the Lord, the answer came so quickly and completely. For the next five years we were to focus on what we called the 40/70 Window (postulating that Ephesus in Turkey was a central headquarters of the Queen of Heaven) and we were to transition from Operation Queen's Palace to Operation Queen's Domain (on the assumption that the Queen of Heaven was primarily responsible for quenching the fires of Christianity in Europe).

How was I able to design this radical transition so rapidly? Even though such a thing might be exactly what is expected from a leader with the gift of apostle, I am convinced I could not have done it were it not for the supporting ministry of the prophets.

Chuck Pierce had heard from the Lord that immediate action was necessary, and he knew how to communicate the message to me in a way that would provoke me to take the necessary steps.

Quite a while before I inquired of the Lord, three intercessors had heard prophetically that my decision should be to transition to the 40/70 Window. The four of them (when you include Chuck), joined by many others as well, were (without telling me) fervently standing in the gap for me so that when I did inquire of the Lord, He would be able to clearly reveal His will to me. I love this because it makes my work as an apostle so much easier and more enjoyable.

If apostles are properly hitched to prophets, if they have established a covenant relationship and if they have agreed to pull together in ministry, a repeatable pattern emerges. It is like a cycle, with five key points. Let us analyze the dynamics of this cycle point by point.

1. THE PROPHET SUBMITS TO THE APOSTLE

When the Bible says that God has given first apostles and second prophets (see 1 Cor. 12:28), it is not establishing a hierarchy. It is, however, setting forth a procedural relationship. It is like the relationship between a baseball pitcher and catcher. The catcher calls the pitch but the pitcher actually throws the ball. Furthermore, the pitcher can and does overrule the catcher's call when necessary. Neither one is considered to have a higher position in the team's hierarchy. Nevertheless, when the game is over, the winning pitcher—not the winning catcher—is the individual who goes into the record books.

What is the bottom line? Over the course of a season, it is the *team*, not an individual pitcher or catcher, that wins the World Series. In fact, it may not be either a pitcher or a catcher, but a center fielder or a first baseman or whomever, who is declared the season's most valuable player. No team wins the World Series, however, unless the pitchers and catchers understand their mutual roles of interdependence. One of those roles is that the catcher is submitted to the pitcher.

I will not forget the first time I spoke on these five points of the apostle-prophet cycle to a group of prophets. When I suggested that prophets begin by submitting to apostles, it seemed like a charge of static electricity swept around the table. Even though everyone maintained an appropriate level of courtesy, I am enough of a communicator to know when my audience is not totally buying into what I am saying.

Naturally, this came up later during the discussion period. Since I am so new at this area of ministry, I do not find myself carrying much of the baggage that veterans, such as those prophets around the table, are carrying. They have been around the block a few times, while I am working on my first trip around. Fortunately, they knew me well enough to understand and excuse my naiveté, and they trusted me enough to let me know why they had problems with the categorical principle that the prophet submits to the apostle.

I learned that there is a residual, knee-jerk distrust of apostles on the part of some prophets. In the last chapter, I quoted Bill Hamon as saying, "Some prophets are getting nervous and concerned about the restoration of apostles and are fearful that they will try to structure them into a restricted realm that God never intended."[1] Such discomfort on the part of some prophets can be traced to at least two causes: the Shepherding Movement and flaky apostles.

The Shepherding Movement

Many prophets (and other Christian leaders as well) are carrying unhealed or partially healed wounds from what was known as the Shepherding Movement or Discipleship Movement of the 1970s. This movement, led by Bob Mumford and others, attained a good bit of notoriety among the fledgling independent charismatic churches of the day. It advocated forming accountability pyramids in which each individual believer displayed faithfulness to God by entering into a covenant relationship of strong submission with another believer called a shepherd. This, among other things, could involve tithing a percentage of their income to the shepherd.

Pat Robertson blew the whistle on the Shepherding Movement in an open letter in 1975. After a period of intense controversy, the movement began to lose force and, for all intents and purposes, has long since moved off the scene. Even Bob Mumford has publicly apologized and renounced the movement. Still, many of the veteran prophets of today have roots in the independent charismatic movement and some were severely burned—either directly or indirectly—by the Shepherding Movement. It is interesting that Pat Robertson, in his open letter, denounced as cultish the Shepherding Movement's use of words like "relationship" and "submission."[2]

During the heyday of the Shepherding Movement, I had my hands full trying to work my way out of a secessionist mind-set in order to embrace the present-day ministry of the Holy Spirit. I was in spiritual elementary school, so to speak. Consequently, I was oblivious to independent charismatics and the Shepherding Movement, and I doubt if I could have identified either Bob Mumford or Pat Robertson in those days. However, I can clearly understand why many survivors of the Shepherding Movement would have a serious problem with the use of the word "submission."

Flaky Apostles

The second major reason why some prophets have a difficult time with the idea of submitting to apostles is that they have tried it and struck out. Even apart from the Shepherding Movement, immature apostles have been known to yield to the temptation of spiritual abuse. Because of the incredible authority that God delegates to apostles, this is a temptation that will never go away. It is Satan's Secret Weapon Number One in his attempt to destroy the apostolic movement. Genuine apostles who are filled with the Holy Spirit and who choose to be holy in all their conduct will not yield to this temptation. Consequently, their authority will be a blessing, not a curse, to their apostolic ministry teams and to their followers.

Nevertheless, there have been flaky apostles. Some of them never had the gift of apostle in the first place. Others may have had the spiritual gift, but they attempted to use it without the fruit of the Spirit. Neither of these courses will work, and those who have been seduced by such apostles, including some prophets, are to be pitied. I cannot blame prophets who have been caught in an abusive situation and who have gone through the trauma of breaking out of it if they say, "Never again!"

Biblical Submission

Understanding some of the abuses of submission in the past does not give us license to throw the baby out with the bathwater. The Bible clearly teaches about divinely ordered submission. Ephesians 5:21 speaks of "submitting to one another in the fear of God." This is in the context of the marriage relationship. How is God's order of mutual submission to be worked out in marriage? Wives are to obey their husbands as the Church obeys Christ, and husbands are to love their wives as Christ loves the Church. True, some husbands abuse their wives like some apostles abuse prophets. This causes some wives to refuse to submit to their husbands and to remove the promise to obey from their marriage vows. But this does not work—it sends the divorce rates off the charts and it pulls the rug out from under the nuclear family. It is a way of throwing the baby out with the bathwater.

As marriage counselors well know, this is rarely *either* the husband's fault *or* the wife's fault. It is most frequently the fault of both because they have not mutually recognized God's appointed order of submitting to one another. The concept of submission is not the root of the difficulty. The root is the failure of the parties involved to submit properly and maturely to each other *in the fear of the Lord.*

Let us apply this biblical principle of submission, according to the order of God, to apostles and prophets. God's order will work as it should if prophets first agree to submit themselves to apostles.

2. GOD SPEAKS TO THE PROPHET

Let me begin this section by quoting my definition of the spiritual gift of prophecy:

> The gift of prophecy is the special ability that God gives to certain members of the Body of Christ to receive and communicate an immediate message of God to His people through a divinely anointed utterance.[3]

Some people have a problem understanding the gift of prophecy because of the fact that every believer, not just a few, has the ability to hear from God. Most of us believe that prayer, for example, is two-way communication. We speak to God in prayer and He also speaks to us. But the fact of the matter is that some of us, day in and day out, are better at hearing God more often and more accurately than others. Why do some not hear as well as others? In some cases, it might be our own fault because we do not try hard enough or because we are not filled with the Holy Spirit or because there is some sin in our lives that is blocking our relationship with God.

The Spiritual Gift of Prophecy and the Office of Prophet

This will explain some cases, but in other cases the reason why some hear so clearly from God is because He has chosen to give them the spiritual gift of prophecy. Not everyone has the gift of prophecy. If we all did, the whole Body would be an eye, and this is impossible (see 1 Cor. 12:17). Only a certain few have the *spiritual gift* of prophecy, while all believers have a common role of hearing from God and prophesying from time to time.

Of those who have the gift of prophecy, a certain few come to be recognized by the Body of Christ as having the office of prophet. They would be included in the list of Ephesians 4:11: "apostles," "prophets," "evangelists," "pastors" and "teachers." It is those with both the *gift* of prophecy and the *office* of prophet who form, along with apostles, the foundation of the Church (see Eph. 2:20).

I mentioned previously that there are two ways apostles receive the revelation from God that translates into a clear vision for where He wants the Church to go. One way is for apostles to receive God's revelation through the prophets and the other way is for apostles to receive revelation directly from God. It seems that God's Plan A is to use prophets for this purpose. The Bible says, "Surely the Lord GOD does nothing, unless He reveals His secret to His servants the prophets" (Amos 3:7). God certainly is not limited by this approach. He can go to a Plan B in order to accomplish His purpose (i.e., giving the revelation directly to apostles). But if God does, it is probably not His best for us, according to Amos 3:7.

Before moving on, let us clarify that Plan A (God speaking through the prophets) will not work as it should unless the prophet submits to the apostle. If there is no apostle in the equation, we end up with another frustrated prophet. I do not know how many prophets I have heard lamenting, "Why won't anyone listen to me?" I would not question whether these individuals are true prophets or whether they have accurately heard from God. They might rate high in both of the above. But the reason few are listening is most likely because the apostle is not there to set things in order so that someone will listen.

3. THE PROPHET SPEAKS TO THE APOSTLE

Once the prophet hears the message of the hour from God, this message must be delivered to the apostle. The better the apostle and the prophet know each other and the better the track record they have in pulling together in ministry, the easier this becomes. In all cases, however, the prophet needs to exercise mature spiritual discernment in speaking the message to the apostle.

There are at least two ways the rhema word of God can come to a prophet. First, it can be a *nabi* type of prophecy that, according to Chuck Pierce, can mean "a supernatural message that bubbles up or springs forth."[4] While they would not be restricted to nabi prophecies, on many occasions I have seen Bill Hamon and Cindy Jacobs, two prophets with whom I am closely associated, receive and speak out this kind of unpremeditated, springing-forth type of word. This comes so rapidly that spur-of-the-moment discernment must be exercised more by spiritual reflex action than by a careful thought process. Nabi is a risky kind of prophecy, especially when it is spoken to apostles or other leaders whose decisions, presumably guided by the prophecy, can affect the lives and destinies of many people.

The second way the word frequently comes is through prophetic intercession. When a prophet has been interceding for an apostle over a period of time, the probability of accuracy in speaking into the life and ministry of that apostle increases proportionately. Furthermore, the process of communicating this kind of word to the apostle allows much more room for mature spiritual discernment. Through my personal experience with prophets and prophecy I have pinpointed two special areas for discernment on the part of the prophet.

What to Tell and What Not to Tell

The prophet needs to decide what to tell the apostle and what not to tell. Some prophetic words are given to prophetic intercessors just so they can stand in the gap for the apostle, and the apostle should not even know about it. On many occasions, I have had a call from one of our personal intercessors with words to the effect: "Peter, I prayed for you from three to six this morning, and God gave me five incredible revelations about you and your ministry. I am allowed to tell you only two of them, and here they are . . ." I am deeply grateful for this kind of discernment. This intercessor is truly a prayer shield. In fact, some of my most powerful personal intercessors communicate with me rarely, if at all.

The Difference Timing Can Make

The second area of discernment has to do with timing. The prophet might receive a word that clearly must be communicated to the apostle, but the question is when. For example, take the case of the three intercessors who had heard from God that I was to transition the global prayer movement from the 10/40 Window to the 40/70 Window. They had communicated the information to each other, but their collective discernment told them they were not to mention it to me until God had given me the word directly. It was Bobbye Byerly, one of our I-2 intercessors, who told me about this in the lunch meeting when I first announced the 40/70 Window transition. And I must say, Bobbye did not attempt to hide her excitement about finally being able to tell me!

Prophets often wish that apostles were not so slow in hearing from God. But prophets need to be patient because the timing is very important. I can well imagine that if I had not been assigned to hear from God directly about the 40/70 Window, some would have probably suspected that I had been unduly swayed by the prophets. Skeptics might have felt I had caved into the opinion of some prophets who might have had hidden agendas that they wanted to co-opt me into endorsing.

To give another example, my number one personal decision in 1999 was to consolidate into one the two ministries I had been heading. Chuck Pierce knew from the beginning of the long process that this was exactly what God wanted me to do. We walked arm in arm through the months of transition, and from time to time Chuck would nudge me with a prophetic word that would invariably be a word in season. When the consolidation was finally over and he told me he had known all along what was going to happen, I said, with a tinge of rebuke, "Why didn't you tell me sooner? You could have saved us months of grief!"

He calmly replied, "Peter, I couldn't tell you because you weren't ready. You would have messed the whole thing up!" This is what I mean by a prophet exercising discernment in timing.

Before we leave this subject, let me just mention in passing that at the point when the prophet speaks the word of the Lord to the apostle, and the apostle receives it, the apostle is submitted to the prophet. This is a further example of "submitting to one another in the fear of God" (Eph. 5:21).

4. THE APOSTLE JUDGES, EVALUATES, STRATEGIZES AND EXECUTES

Once the prophetic word is given, now the burden for serious discernment switches from the prophet to the apostle. Only foolish apostles would receive and act on every prophetic word sent in their direction. As I have said, I only enter a small percentage of the total number of prophetic words I receive into my *Prophetic Journal.* When it comes to spontaneous nabi words, the percentage entered into the journal is extremely low. The numbers are low even for those words spoken at highly intense moments in a meeting where there is laying on of hands, extravagant affirmation by those gathered around and a tape recording made. Most of these cases, which are not infrequent, involve what I have called Paul-Agabus relationships, rather than Paul-Silas relationships.

I feel it is my personal responsibility to judge prophecies that come my way. In many cases I am judging the prophecy as it is given, and halfway through I know that the Holy Spirit, who has filled me, is not allowing me to bear witness to it. For example, when the person speaking declares that I will be consulted by kings and presidents and prime ministers, which occasionally occurs, I rather quickly tune out. It is God who works in me to *will* and to do His good pleasure (see Phil. 2:13), and I know that He has not given me any more desire (or will) to meet politicians than to work in a coal mine the rest of my life. So I have learned to be courteous through situations like this. When the person finishes, I say, "Thank you. Praise the Lord!" and I accept the recording of the prophecy.

Not Taking Offense

One of the reasons I am describing my personal discernment process is because I want prophets to know that apostles must judge their words and filter out those that do not apply. Prophets should not feel offended by this process. It does not necessarily mean that the words filtered out are not accurate; in some cases, the timing could be off. It is very important to remember that at this point, the burden for dealing with the word of the Lord is on the apostle, and no longer the prophet. There have been and will continue to be many occasions when the apostle should have received and acted on a certain prophetic word but did not. In cases like this, it is the apostle who is responsible before the Lord for missing the prophecy, not the prophet who delivered it.

Once apostles accept words as being valid for the moment, a process of evaluation begins. Bill Hamon says, "However it may be worded, a personal prophecy will always be *partial, progressive,* and *conditional.*"[5] Among other things, he bases this on 1 Corinthians 13:9, "For we know in part and we prophesy in part." These three factors will enter into the process of evaluation. Moreover, apostles are not necessarily expected to do this evaluation in isolation from others. In many cases apostles will enter into a period of consultation with other key players, including prophets, in order to make sure they understand the word.

Evaluating Stock Market Prophecies

As a personal illustration of this, one of the prophets with whom I associate had a word in 1998 that the stock market would go down in June and begin to go back up in September. My retirement funds, important to Doris and me in this stage of life, are in a self-directed plan in which I can move them in and out of the stock market with an automated phone call. I had a lot of these funds in the stock market in 1998, so I took them out in late July and put them back in late September. As a result, I made the equivalent of a generous year's salary.

I evaluated that one pretty well. But in 1999 this same person had a word that the stock market would change on September 18 and move again on October 18. I did not evaluate that prophetic word well because I thought it meant that the market would take a nose dive on October 18, so I stayed out of the market for the rest of the year. In this case, I did not lose anything, but if I had interpreted the move on October 18 as going up, my retirement funds would be worth a lot more at this writing.

Why do I bring up such a mundane subject? For one thing it is because my action in this case affected no one except Doris and me—no big deal. Also, I have heard many other prophecies about finances, some of which predicted that the entire world banking system would collapse before the end of the last millennium, and none of them caused me to take any personal action. Why did I act on these? It was because of the Paul-Silas type of relationship that had developed with this person over the years.

Setting Things in Order

When the prophecy has been judged and evaluated, it is time for action. This is where an apostle's primary anointing kicks in. Paul wrote to Titus, "I left you in Crete, that you should *set in order* the things that are lacking" (Titus 1:5, emphasis mine). Developing a strategy and executing the plan are what apostles do best. It does not always mean that they keep hands-on control of what happens, although sometimes it is necessary. At this point there is much room for team building and delegation.

I do not need to elaborate on this because what apostles do was thoroughly covered in earlier chapters. To summarize, apostles are very pragmatic. They do what it takes to accomplish the will of God in a particular job and to ensure that the job is done well.

5. THE PROPHET SUBMITS TO THE APOSTLE

I said in the beginning that these five points are on a cycle. Therefore, no explanation is needed of this point, because it is the same as point number one.

SATURATION HUMILITY

A final note in the examination of how apostles are hitched to prophets is the need to recognize the role of humility in a healthy relationship between these top leaders. In the horse pull we talked about at the beginning of the chapter, it is interesting that the 2,000-pound horses are submitted to a 180-pound teamster. Humility is important for championship draft animals to have.

But humility is even more important for apostles and prophets. Those of us who are recognized as apostles and prophets need to know ourselves well enough to be conscious of the fact that we have been "exalted" by God. By this I do not mean that we will necessarily receive more rewards in heaven at the judgment seat of Christ. But I do mean that here on Earth we have been given much more responsibility than the average believer. We have a higher visibility. Many people whom we do not know feel that they know us well. We are on the platform and they are in the audience. We write the books, they read them. We are household names within our apostolic spheres.

God has made us the foundation of the Church (see Eph. 2:20). Stating this is not a lack of humility. It is thinking soberly of ourselves, as we are told to do in Romans 12:3, and striving to live up to the enormous responsibility that it entails.

Jesus said, "Whoever exalts himself will be humbled, and he who humbles himself will be exalted" (Matt. 23:12). If we take this statement literally, and I see no reason why we should not, we must conclude that we are humble, even though we might do so reluctantly. If we were not humble, Jesus Himself says that we would not be exalted. By this I do not mean that we should ever stop striving to be more humble than we are now. I would not deny that the temptation of pride is always lurking just around the corner and that from time to time we can and do fall into that sin. But just as certainly, if we were not characterized—day by day, week by week—by a lifestyle of genuine humility, we would not be authentic apostles and prophets.

Humility is implicit in everything I have said in this chapter. But let me be a bit more explicit. Notice that in this process of being hitched and pulling together, the apostles humble themselves to the prophets. Apostles do not go around proclaiming, "I'm the man of God in charge of this ministry and if God wants to speak to us, He will speak through me." No, a true apostle will say, "I'm not the only one who hears from God for this ministry." That is humility.

The prophets, in turn, humble themselves before the apostles. They do not try to control the way the apostles interpret and execute the words they have received. This is humility, because many times the prophet "knows" that the apostle is on the wrong track. In the apostle-prophet relationships that have gone sour, often a chief contributing factor is a lack of humility on the part of prophets who overstep their boundaries and try to do what the apostles are supposed to do. Genuine prophets realize that if the apostle makes a mistake, it is not the prophet's fault.

Apostles and prophets can change the world if they are properly hitched to each other and if they are able to pull together!

Notes

1. Dr. Bill Hamon, *Apostles, Prophets and the Coming Moves of God* (Shippensburg, PA: Destiny Image, 1997), p. 139

2. Harold D. Hunter, "Shepherding Movement," *Dictionary of Pentecostal and Charismatic Movements*, eds. Stanley M. Burgess and Gary B. McGee (Grand Rapids, MI: Zondervan Publishing House, 1988), p. 784.

3. C. Peter Wagner, *Your Spiritual Gifts Can Help Your Church Grow*, rev. ed. (Ventura, CA: Regal Books, 1994), p. 229.

4. Chuck D. Pierce and Rebecca Wagner Sytsema, *Receiving the Word of the Lord* (Colorado Springs: Wagner Publications, 1999), p. 15.

5. Dr. Bill Hamon, *Prophets and Personal Prophecy* (Shippensburg, PA: Destiny Image, 1987), p. 145.

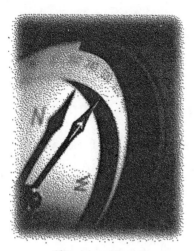

Chapter Seven

APOSTLES AND PROPHETS IN REAL LIFE

From time to time I have been sharing personal illustrations of how apostles can relate to prophets and vice versa. In this chapter I am going to share a few more for two main reasons. First, I am personally involved in each of the situations that I will bring up, and therefore I have a good vantage point from which to interpret and analyze what has taken place. Second, several real-life examples of bad experiences with prophecy have been surfacing recently, and I want to help balance the picture by entering several good ones into the public record. I am not saying that the examples of bad experiences with prophecy are necessarily inaccurate. I just want to say that at these relatively early stages of the resurgent prophetic movement, we have a mixed bag on our hands. There are some really good things going on, and there are also some things that we hope will soon be corrected as the movement itself matures.

STRATEGIC-LEVEL SPIRITUAL WARFARE

I have already mentioned that I was a frequent visitor to the Vineyard Christian Fellowship of Anaheim, California, throughout the 1980s. One of my visits occurred in 1990, soon after the Kansas City Prophets had begun ministering there. Doris and I were in John Wimber's office drinking diet soda during one of their conferences. All of a sudden John said to Todd Hunter, then one of Wimber's closest associates, "Go get John Paul Jackson!" We had never heard of John Paul Jackson, but it turned out that he was a well-known member of the Kansas City Prophets.

When the prophet came into the office, John introduced us. After the normal formalities, John said, "John Paul, do you have a word for Peter and Doris?" We were not used to things like that as yet, especially when Jackson looked at us, paused for a moment and softly said, "Yes." This was an instance of what I have described as a Paul-Agabus relationship.

The question going through my mind was *How could he have a word for us if he has just met us? He doesn't know anything about us.* In fact, his prophecy was among the first that we received, and it is actually on page 3 of our *Prophetic Journal*! At that moment, we were definitely being pushed toward the fringe of our comfort zone!

Among other things, John Paul said to me:

You are now about to face the greatest challenge of your life. You are being called to help reshape the face of Christianity. You will be placed in an international arena which will begin in South America.

Even before the magnitude of what John Paul Jackson had said began to filter down, I was questioning in my mind the "South America" part of it. Although Doris and I had ministered in South America—Bolivia to be exact—for 16 years, my ministry in South America had been minimal since our departure in 1971. As John Paul was prophesying, I began searching my brain for a recollection of any invitation I had received to South America, and I could recall none. I did know that I had an invitation to Mexico, however. This caused me to begin to rationalize and suspect that perhaps John Paul did not realize that Mexico was not located in South America. There was no chance to discuss it at the moment, so I just let it be for a time.

It was only a very short time afterward that Ed Silvoso of Harvest Evangelism in Argentina had a meeting with me and we agreed to launch an annual Harvest Evangelism International Institute in Argentina. Silvoso and I also agreed to run a large-scale experiment in strategic-level spiritual warfare in the city of Resistencia (in northern Argentina). This set in place one of my major courses for the decade of the 1990s, putting me on the front lines of field-based, evangelism-oriented prayer and spiritual warfare for many years.

One of the results of the alliance with Ed Silvoso was the release of the six-volume Prayer Warrior series.[1] At this writing, that series of books has circulated more than 350,000 copies in English and has been translated into at least 11 other languages. John Paul Jackson's prophecy had stated that this phase of my life would begin in South America. Well, here is the first sentence of the first chapter of the first volume of the series, *Warfare Prayer*: "Argentina is a good beginning scenario to explain what warfare prayer is all about."[2] Argentina *is* in South America, so there was no confusion of terms in God's revelation to John Paul Jackson.

I do not think this intense involvement in strategic-level spiritual warfare was the entire scope of the word that I would be called to help "reshape the face of Christianity." But it was definitely one important component of the total thing that God had in mind. In this new millennium, the Body of Christ worldwide is much more aware of—and much better equipped to wrestle against—principalities and powers than ever before in recorded Church history. And the accelerated process started around 1990, the year of John Paul Jackson's prophecy. Let me hasten to say that the Holy Spirit was speaking the same message about strategic-level spiritual warfare to many other leaders at the time, not just to me. But I did, and still do, have the privilege of serving as the international coordinator of the Spiritual Warfare Network.

THE GLOBAL PRAYER MOVEMENT

Occasionally I am faced with a decision that I do not feel I should make until my intercessors have had the opportunity to pray it through and hear what God might want to say to me through them. Remember that a large percentage of the prophetic words I receive from God come through my personal intercessors.

Such was the case in 1991 when Luis Bush, international director of the AD2000 and Beyond Movement, invited me to take the position of coordinator of his AD2000 United Prayer Track. At the time, I was fully aware that accepting this responsibility would probably change the primary focus of my career for years to come. So I inquired of the Lord and sent out a prayer alert to our I-1 and

I-2 intercessors. In fact, I had told Luis that my decision would be greatly affected by what response I received from the intercessors. To be truthful, at that time I was not totally convinced that the AD2000 Movement itself was really the will of God, but that is another story (and I have since changed my mind).

Just as a parenthetical point of interest, on a later occasion I was invited by the publishing company Thomas Nelson to be the general editor of a major study Bible on spiritual warfare. At the time, I was leaning toward accepting the responsibility. But again, I told the publisher that my decision would be based largely upon what God would reveal to my intercessors about the project. When I sent the word out, I received a tepid to negative response. That was enough for me to say, "Thanks, but no thanks!" Since then, I do not know how many times I have been extremely thankful for that decision because I now know the project would have been a major distraction from what God really wanted me to do.

Such was definitely not the case for the AD2000 United Prayer Track. When I sent that word out, the intercessors broke all previous records in responding not only with rapidity but with enthusiastic affirmation. They left no room for saying, "Thanks, but no thanks!" For example, this is what Alice Smith, our I-1 intercessor at the time, wrote:

I feel the glory of the Lord around AD2000. It's not like anything else I've ever felt. When I pray for it, the Lord descends on me big time! Whatever this movement is, get on it. I don't really understand what it is all about, and maybe that's good. Even though I don't know much about it, I know you should be in on it. God comes so powerfully every time I mention it! This is a God-ordained program! It is where God is moving right now!

THE WORLD PRAYER CENTER

Needless to say, I called Luis Bush and accepted the position. Sure enough, our ministry through the 1990s was largely molded by the AD2000 United Prayer Track. It was through AD2000, for example, that Doris and I first met Ted Haggard of New Life Church and bonded with him in a covenant relationship to build the World Prayer Center in Colorado Springs. In 1998 we dedicated the 55,000-square-foot facility, which has now become a high-tech hub for intercessors all over the world to keep in touch with each other.

Then I remembered an impromptu prophecy that Cindy Jacobs gave me in my kitchen in our home in Altadena, California, drinking coffee with a group of our personal intercessors. This was one of her nabi, or "bubbling forth," prophecies. Among other things, she said,

> *The Lord would say that the ministry of Global Harvest Ministries will widen far beyond what you and Doris have planned or anticipated. It will not end when the AD2000 United Prayer Track is terminated, but it will continue into the future. It will grow to such proportions that you will have a building of your own.*

My immediate response was not even to put this into our *Prophetic Journal*, because our plan was to phase out the Prayer Track when the AD2000 Movement ceased in the year 2000. A building of our own?! No such thought had ever entered our minds. But, true to form, it turned out to be a directive word for us, and I have definitely inserted it into its proper place in the *Prophetic Journal*, where it should have been all along! Although the United Prayer Track is now a thing of the past, we are comfortably settled in our own building, the World Prayer Center, and we are helping to expand the global prayer movement far beyond what we were able to do in the 1990s.

BILL HAMON'S PHOENIX PROPHECY

While I have a Paul-Silas relationship with Alice Smith and Cindy Jacobs because they are two of our long-term personal intercessors, another very significant prophecy that came through Bishop Bill Hamon can be seen as a Paul-Agabus type of prophecy.

This occurred in Phoenix in 1992. Our friend Hal Sacks, who was hosting us in an event there, told us that Bill and Evelyn Hamon of Christian International were in town and wanted to meet us. Now, Bill Hamon was one of my heroes because, as I have mentioned, his book *Prophets and Personal Prophecy* was the first thing I had read on the subject that made sense to me, and it had set the whole concept of prophetic ministry in order to my satisfaction. I actually never thought I would have the privilege of meeting such a figure as Bill Hamon. I did not think that "Bishop," as his friends call him, even knew I existed. Doris and I immediately made an appointment and went to meet him.

Bill and Evelyn were in a hotel room, and when we entered we saw a tape recorder on the table. Did this mean that he was actually going to prophesy? It did, and the prophecy takes up no less than three single-spaced pages in our *Prophetic Journal*! Here is part of what Dr. Hamon said:

> *"The work that I've called you to do over the next 10 years,"* saith God, *"will be more productive and more effective than all the rest of your life put together. You are going to begin to touch new leaders, and the leaders you touch are going to touch hundreds, and the hundreds are going to touch thousands, and the*

thousands are going to touch millions. I'm going to use you to
cause a chain reaction," saith God. "I've not called you to speak
to the multitudes, I've called you to speak to My key leaders."

THE NEW APOSTOLIC REFORMATION

A few months after this I began to research what I have chosen
to call the New Apostolic Reformation. When Bill Hamon
prophesied, I had not realized that the apostolic movement—as
a movement—even existed. However, in 1993 it was almost from
one day to the next that God began to show me the commonal-
ities of the movement as well as its immense importance as a
new wineskin to carry the Church into the twenty-first century.
I now see that this is, in all probability, the heart of the outcome
of the prophecy from John Paul Jackson that I would be called to
"help reshape the face of Christianity." Since then, this has been
the primary focus of my research, teaching and writing. My
books *The New Apostolic Churches* and *Churchquake!* were the first
two to emerge from my new assignment, and this book is the
third.

MOVING FROM CALIFORNIA
TO COLORADO

In 1992, Doris and I had planned our retirement. When I had finished teaching at Fuller Seminary and when the AD2000
Movement had closed down, we were going to enjoy the rest of our
lives in our comfortable home in Altadena, California, at the foot of
the majestic San Gabriel Mountains, where we had lived since 1971.

However, while we were in the hotel room in Phoenix, Bill Hamon went on to prophesy:

Your financial affairs are in My hands, and I'm about to give you a better, different place of your permanent residence and of your permanent headquarters where you can reside; a more spacious, roomier place. It's going to be given to you.

Well, here we are. Since 1996 we have lived in our spacious, custom-designed home in the Black Forest area of Colorado Springs. I must say that I liked the "It's going to be given to you" part of the prophecy really well, and I was applying it to my house. However, I ended up saddled with a large mortgage! So I decided that I would tease Bill Hamon and ask him why, in the light of his Phoenix prophecy, I had a big mortgage on my hands.

Without hesitating, he said, "Peter, I don't think you understand prophetic language well enough. Go back and read it again." Consequently, I exegeted the prophecy, and as you can see, the object of "to be given" could be either the "permanent residence" or the "permanent headquarters." Well the "permanent headquarters," the World Prayer Center, was truly given to us through the generosity of many donors and New Life Church. And to be truthful, I have not had difficulty making the mortgage payments on my home.

WAGNER LEADERSHIP INSTITUTE

I was ordained to the Christian ministry in 1955, when I was 25 years old. However, I feel that my real career began in 1998, when I was 68 years old. That was when I resigned from Fuller Seminary after teaching for 31 years in the School of World

Mission and started a school of my own, Wagner Leadership Institute. What precipitated this radical, late-life change?

On June 6, 1998, a group of friends had gathered in our living room to celebrate Chuck Pierce's birthday. The candles had been blown out and some were cutting and distributing the birthday cake when all of a sudden, Cindy Jacobs got a look on her face with which I had become quite familiar. She stared into space and said, "The spirit of prophecy is so strong!" I suggested that she relax for a moment while we found a tape recorder. Prophesying had not been on our original agenda!

BIGGER THAN IMAGINATION

When we had the tape recorder going, it turned out that the first part of the prophecy was for me. She went on and on. What she said actually takes up two pages in our *Prophetic Journal*. I was concentrating as hard as I could, but to be honest, nothing she was saying was making any sense. I had no mental hooks to hang it on. Here are some excerpts:

> For the Lord would say, "I am going to build a seminary here in Colorado Springs. I am going to gather leaders from around the world. There are going to be extensions of this seminary that will go forth into the nations of the world." And the Lord says, "My son, the curriculum that I am going to put together in this school is like nothing that has been seen before. It is going to happen quickly. The Wagner Institute is so big that you cannot imagine how big it is. For it is greater than anything you could ever dream of."

That last line was very accurate. It had never even entered my mind to start a school of any kind. I had informed Fuller Seminary that I would teach my last class in 2000, just before I turned 70. After that I thought I would do a bit of teaching in some of the schools of the New Apostolic Reformation while I was collecting Social Security and easing into retirement. But as far as Cindy's prophecy was concerned, I had it transcribed, prayed about it for a couple of days and then practically forgot about it because it still did not make any sense to me. I was getting no further revelation from God in the slightest. In fact, it seemed so far out that I did not even send it to our I-1 and I-2 intercessors for scrutiny, although a few of them were present at the birthday party.

GETTING TO BE AN OLD MAN!

Things suddenly changed a month later, on July 17. We were in the same living room, but this time with a small group of apostles and other leaders who had come to town to take one of my Fuller Seminary courses. Rice Broocks was there, along with David Cannistraci, Lawrence Khong, Joe Martin, Dexter Low, Kay Hiramine, Cindy and Mike Jacobs and perhaps others. We were eating pizza and just hanging out. At one point, I casually mentioned that down the road, after I left Fuller, I hoped to be able to teach in some of their new apostolic schools. That prompted Dexter Low, from Malaysia, to say:

> *Peter, how old are you?* [I responded that I was 68; he went on.] *You don't have very many years of ministry left. Do you mean that you are going to spend the two best years of the rest of your life just coasting along and then give the leftovers to us?*

I italicized what Dexter said because, although it was not purported to be a prophecy per se, it immediately spoke to my heart as if it were a direct word from God. Same difference! Everyone else was silent, looking at me. I said, "That sounds like you are suggesting I should resign from Fuller Seminary!"

Rice Broocks then looked at Doris and said, "Doris, what do you think?"

She said, "I told him he should have left Fuller three years ago so he could retire at 65!"

That was enough for me. I said, "OK, I'll write my letter of resignation tomorrow." And I did! It was to take effect on September 1, when my annual contract would come up for renewal.

Whereas no revelation concerning the Wagner Leadership Institute (WLI) had been forthcoming at all previously, the instant I signed that letter God began to speak so rapidly to me day after day that I could hardly keep up and write it all down. I had the basic elements of the philosophy of education, the structure, the curriculum, the student body, the faculty, the administration and the catalog for WLI together before I could hardly come up for air. One advantage I had was that by then I understood apostolic leadership. That means I did not have to seek approval of what God was showing me from faculties or faculty senates or academic affairs committees or accrediting associations or boards of trustees. I did plenty of consultation, but the final decisions were mine.

EMANUELE CANNISTRACI HAD TOLD ME

Actually, I should have read my *Prophetic Journal* more. If I had, I might have remembered a prophecy from Emanuele Cannistraci two years previously, in 1996. He said:

*I'm going to give you strength, I'm going to give you an extended life, O man of God. You are needed. **When you break from your present position as professor and instructor,** you are going to be a pastor to pastors, an apostolic leader to a whole new breed of men and women. The latter house is going to be greater than the former.*

Obviously this explains why I received no revelation from God concerning WLI until the day I resigned from Fuller.

When I read the WLI catalog, I still stand amazed at the dynamic and strategic shape this school has taken. We are able to provide earned diplomas at associate, bachelor, master and doctoral levels without academic requirements. The faculty members are successful apostles, prophets, evangelists, pastors and teachers. Their assignment in WLI is not so much to transfer information but to impart vision and anointing for ministry to the students. Therefore, we need neither exams nor grades. Students are all currently active in ministry. They are selected and placed on the basis of age, maturity and ministry experience, not academic degrees. Their median age is around the mid-forties. I know of no other training institution exactly like it.

APPLYING THE FIVE-POINT CYCLE

Let me be very explicit about how the process that sparked WLI illustrates the relationship between apostles and prophets. In this case, I was the apostle and Cindy Jacobs was the main prophet. This was a Paul-Silas type of relationship. Cindy never could have written our WLI catalog. That is not her gifting. And I never could have come up with the two-page birthday party prophecy. That is not my gifting. To flash back to the five points of the apostle-prophet cycle explained in the last chapter, here is how it worked in real life:

1. Cindy submitted to me. She even has written in her books that I serve as her mentor and her spiritual dad. I am on her Generals of Intercession Board of Directors. Using the term "apostle" is perhaps too new to appear in a book, but someday it may. She will tell you that she recognizes my spiritual authority when necessary.

2. God spoke to Cindy. At the birthday party she said, "The spirit of prophecy is so strong!"

3. Cindy spoke to me. I tape recorded and transcribed what she said.

4. I implemented it and became the founding chancellor of Wagner Leadership Institute.

5. Cindy submitted to me. In fact, she is now a core faculty member and the coordinator of both the Prophecy Concentration and the Women in Ministry Concentration of WLI.

In summary, I am acutely aware that I would not have been afforded the same level of effectiveness in ministry if I had not been opened by the Holy Spirit to receive the directive words from the Lord that have come to me through His prophets. "Believe in the LORD your God, and you shall be established; believe His prophets, and you shall prosper" (2 Chron. 20:20).

Notes
1. This series is published by Regal Books, Ventura, California, U.S.A., and includes the following titles: *Warfare Prayer, Prayer Shield, Breaking Strongholds in Your City, Churches That Pray, Confronting the Powers* and *Praying with Power.*
2. C. Peter Wagner, *Warfare Prayer* (Ventura, CA: Regal Books, 1992), p. 15.

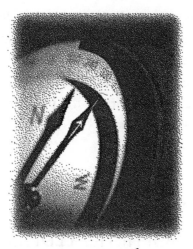

Chapter Eight

APOSTOLIC ORDER IN THE PROPHETIC MOVEMENT

In the last chapter, I gave several examples showing how as an apostle I have benefited greatly through the direct ministry of prophets in my life. In this chapter, I am going to try to illustrate how the reverse is also true: Prophets can better be what God wants them to be if they agree to become hitched to apostles for the long haul.

I am well aware that this chapter is a risky venture, but it is a calculated risk on my part. I am going to try to describe the process that led a number of nationally recognized prophets to take two steps: first, to form a unique association; second, to look to me as the apostle providing leadership for the group. It is risky, first because the story will be so personal. It is also risky because this is such a new venture that the jury is still out as to how functional it will actually be and for how long. However, I see such a high potential for this group—and dozens of similar groups forming here in America and all over the world—that I feel I should include the report in this book. I believe it has the potential to raise the integrity of the prophetic movement in general practically off the charts.

THE APOSTOLIC COUNCIL OF PROPHETIC ELDERS

The association I am referring to, the Apostolic Council of Prophetic Elders (ACPE), was established in Colorado Springs on June 30, 1999. At that time a group of 13 prophets decided to form an accountability structure and they asked me to serve them as a form of apostolic covering. This type of apostle-prophet covering is not yet a common occurrence. Therefore, the best way I know to explain it is through a personal, firsthand narration of some of the ingredients that were mixed into the process.

Such an event raises several questions:

1. What brought about this meeting of prophets?
In September 1998, during a Building Foundations for Revival conference in St. Louis, Cindy Jacobs called a small group of prophets together for lunch. The purpose was to discuss possible ways and means to build relationships and establish mutual accountability among the major recognized prophetic voices in America. Among those present were Chuck Pierce, Bill Hamon, Jim Laffoon and Mike and Cindy Jacobs. I was invited to join them

as an observer. The participants were unanimous in their desire to form some kind of grouping of prophets. Cindy suggested that since a National School of the Prophets had been scheduled to meet at New Life Church in Colorado Springs the following January, an invitation-only meeting of prophets could be convened the day before, on January 27, 1999, in the World Prayer Center.

Cindy asked me to coconvene this group with her, and 18 individuals attended. The consensus of those who participated was that the group should be brought together again as soon as possible. Cindy Jacobs again took the initiative to contact key members and set the date for the next meeting for June 30, 1999, again at the World Prayer Center. She suggested that this time I come not simply as an observer but in more of an apostolic role. In January, I would not have been ready for that suggestion. However, by June, I had begun to understand more concretely what my function as a horizontal apostle was turning out to be, and I was beginning to learn what my God-appointed apostolic spheres would be.

Attendees at the June 30 meeting included Beth Alves (Bulverde, TX), Jim Goll (Nashville, TN), Chuck Pierce (Colorado Springs, CO), Mike and Cindy Jacobs (Colorado Springs, CO), Bart Pierce (Baltimore, MD), John and Paula Sandford (Hayden Lake, ID), Dutch Sheets (Colorado Springs, CO), Tommy Tenney (Pineville, LA), Hector Torres (Colorado Springs, CO), C. Peter Wagner (Colorado Springs, CO) and Barbara Wentroble (Dallas, TX).

2. Who are the prophets committed to the Apostolic Council of Prophetic Elders?

All of the above are charter members, plus Mike Bickle (Kansas City, KS), Paul Cain (Kansas City, KS), Emanuele Cannistraci

(San Jose, CA), Bill Hamon (Santa Rosa Beach, FL), Kingsley Fletcher (Research Triangle Park, NC), Ernest Gentile (San Jose, CA), Jim Laffoon (Rancho Palos Verdes, CA), James Ryle (Longmont, CO) and Gwen Shaw (Jasper, AK).

3. What is the purpose of ACPE?

The prophets decided to organize ACPE in order to build positive and ongoing personal relationships among nationally recognized prophetic voices. They wanted to encourage mutual accountability and establish agreed-upon guidelines for releasing public prophetic declarations, particularly those with the potential of having widespread national or regional implications.

The ACPE is designed to establish high levels of public credibility and widely acknowledged integrity in the ministry of public prophecy. It is hoped that standards of excellence will be set not only for this generation of prophets but also for generations to come. I believe the ACPE will be used by God to create an environment in which what He desires to speak through the prophets will be heard, received and acted upon as a normal part of the lifestyle of the Church.

4. Who decides that someone like me should serve as the apostle of an entity such as ACPE?

As I have explained in previous chapters, God should be the one who initiates the process and calls the person whom He wishes to take leadership. But it is equally important that the major players in an unfolding scenario such as ACPE hear and understand God's initiative clearly enough to take personal ownership. Prophets, by definition, are supposed to hear the voice of God better than average believers. Therefore, it would be expected that prophets would rapidly come to a consensus in recognizing an apostle whom God had chosen for their own organization, which was the case with ACPE.

RECEIVING THE APOSTOLIC ASSIGNMENT

Keep in mind that apostolic authority is never *taken*; it is always *given*. In the formation of the Apostolic Council of Prophetic Elders, my role was not to decide that I would like to be the apostle, as if I were running for some office, but simply to receive what the prophets felt God was saying to them. The prophets *gave* me the apostolic office.

Obviously, none of this would have come to pass if I were not ready to accept the apostolic office that the prophets offered me. But since the whole process seemed to be orchestrated by God, it would be expected that He would have prepared me to assume the responsibility, and He had.

How did this happen?

The National School of the Prophets

The process of my receiving the apostolic office began during the National School of the Prophets in January 1999. Naturally, the ministry of personal prophecy was an important feature of this significant gathering. Before they left, a large number of the 3,000 or so participants received personal tape-recorded words from God through a large and well-organized prophetic presbytery. Impressive numbers of positive testimonies have continued to stream into our offices ever since.

John Wimber's Mantle

Because I was the convener of the School of the Prophets, Doris and I had the privilege of sharing meals with the prophets in a private room during the event. At one of those meals, a spirit of prophecy fell, and many of the prophets gathered around the two of us, speaking God's words into our lives. When transcribed, these prophecies actually occupied 11 pages in our *Prophetic Journal*!

Here are excerpts which, I can now see, related directly to my subsequent apostolic role in the forthcoming Apostolic Council of Prophetic Elders. They were all given on January 29, 1999.

Chuck Pierce said:

> *Peter, I sense the Lord moving those who were birthed and connected with John Wimber under you. You will father and promote their message until it is in its next level of fullness. "And I say to you, I am going to bring to fullness those things that were even released that you were a part of in the early '80s, even that which John Wimber released. I say to you, you will now bring this to fullness, for I will transfer those that he imparted into where the fullness did not arise, [and] you will now begin to adopt and to see that fullness occur," saith the Lord.*

Kingsley Fletcher said:

> *But God says, "I am going to get your hands dirty, and you will do things that will make you say, 'Why am I doing this? Why should I do this?' You will do it, so get ready!"*

Jim Goll said:

> *As others have addressed the matter of John Wimber, I've just been weeping—weeping over hearing the stories because I too lived through*

those times. This may be very peculiar to state, but I see a picture of clouds over you and a balcony in the clouds. I see a person leaning over the balcony and looking down at you. His name is John, and he says, "Take the baton and run with it; run with it for I give you the baton. I did my part and I blew a sound whereby the prophetic noise was heard around the earth. Now I say that you must run the race with endurance for the race is not finished. I give you a baton with which you must run and call forth the apostolic community."

Mike Bickle said:

The Lord showed me, Peter, that you are like unto your good friend John Wimber. The Lord used him with a father's spirit to facilitate ministries that were critical in a certain hour. Yours is not the same because John had his own calling and anointing. But, similar to John's ministry, there is going to be a gathering, a facilitating of fathers and sons. Some of the sons will be 20, some will be 40, some will be 60. Some of the fathers will be young. But they will gather as eagles. The Lord has used you and John as a voice to gather eagles. There will be a government spirit bringing a balance between liberty and order. This combines the freshness of liberty with the preservation of soundness that comes with divine order. The Lord will give you understanding as to how to facilitate this; it is a government gift. We can call it apostolic, we can call it facilitating, we can call it governing, we can call it fathering. You are going to bring together networks. You are going to be a network of networks.

FLOWING WITH THE PROPHECY

As I have explained previously, during most of my 45-plus years of active ministry, I would have had no idea what to do with prophecies like these. This is undoubtedly the basic explanation of why God did not give such prophetic words to me in the past. They would have fallen on deaf ears. However, at this point in 1999 I was ready to receive this message of apostolic direction, pray over it, have others pray with me, ask the Lord to show me how to move ahead and give it my best shot. I was willing to experiment.

It is true that in this season a considerable number of experiments with prophecy have been spurious, particularly the more detailed and measurable personal and corporate prophecies that begin with "Thus saith the Lord." Some of these questionable prophetic utterances have provoked leaders like John Bevere—who himself believes in and receives personal prophecy—to research and write on some abuses of prophecy. His book *Thus Saith the Lord?* has served as a wake-up call to some prophets who have been careless in the ways they have chosen to speak out what they hear from the Lord.

Even Ted Haggard, prominent author and pastor of New Life Church in Colorado Springs, has blown the whistle with a *Ministries Today* column entitled "Do the Prophets Really Know?" He says, "Too many of our leaders are developing a history of false predictions of doom," and he gives several examples. He says, "I trusted the Christian prophets of the day, but in many cases their prophetic utterances were, simply put, wrong."[1]

I have not seen any warnings about flaky prophecy raised in these and other recent writings that have not been thoroughly and openly dealt with in books written by some of the ACPE members. Such books include Bill Hamon's *Prophets, Pitfalls and Principles* and *Prophets and Personal Prophecy* and Cindy Jacobs's *The Voice of God.*

Chuck Pierce, for example, says, "There are false prophets. That is why we are admonished to test all things and hold onto what is good." He then lists seven "unclean sources of prophetic words that we need to be aware of."[2] Following that, he adds, "How do you know if what is being said is from God? How do we test prophecy?" He goes on to discuss 14 different ways that a given prophecy should be tested before the hearer seeks to apply it.[3]

It is clear, then, that both insiders and outsiders are striving to improve the overall quality of prophetic ministry. Remember that we are dealing with a movement that only began to surface around 20 years ago. I believe I am right in observing that many more people are prophesying now than before. Also, as the movement has matured, the occurrence of flaky prophecy is now considerably less than it was not too long ago. This is not to excuse these blunders, but admittedly, many of us are truly beginners in all of this. I would hope there would be some room for leniency toward those who have good hearts but who still have much to learn about flowing with true prophecy.

LET'S NOT BE SPECTATORS

I would see myself in the group that tries to extend grace to the burgeoning prophetic movement. However, I do not want to be a mere spectator, just watching others flow with the prophetic movement. Much less would I want to be a critic, highlighting the errors and the obviously painful experiences that some have had with immature prophets. Rather, I tend to look at prophetic ministries in a positive light, expecting God to use prophets in my own life and ministry to help me hear what the Spirit is saying to the churches. This was my underlying frame of mind as I was listening to the massive number of personal prophecies spoken over Doris and me at the National School of the Prophets.

I must confess, however, that as I heard these prophecies and later read and reread the 11 pages of transcripts, I could not at all comprehend how I would be able to receive and implement John Wimber's mantle of drawing together the prophets. In retrospect, I now see that a major reason for my doubt was I had not as yet understood enough about my personal calling and office of apostle. I knew by then (January 1999) that God had given me the gift of apostle. Still, I could not talk about it or act on it because I was only just beginning to understand the difference between the ministries of *horizontal* apostles and *vertical* apostles.

Nevertheless, I took these prophecies very seriously and began praying sincerely that God would show me what to do with them. He answered this prayer over a period of time. First, he allowed me to realize that as an apostle who was not suspected in the least of having an accompanying gift of prophecy, I could function in a quite nonthreatening way among the prophets. God then began giving me direct revelation as to how forms and order of government could be established among prophets, if they were disposed to receiving my apostolic ministry. I therefore began jotting down some notes that I would use in the June 30, 1999, meeting Cindy Jacobs was convening, if the opportunity presented itself for me to say something.

"LOOK AT THE HISTORY OF THE VINEYARD"

During this same period I sensed God saying to me, *"Look at the history of the Vineyard."* Frankly, I had all but forgotten that Bill Jackson, a Vineyard pastor, had sent me a manuscript of his new book, *The Quest for the Radical Middle: A History of the Vineyard.* In fact, I received my copy of the published book just hours before completing the first draft of this chapter. Because of my close personal relationship with John Wimber, I was very much aware of the general outlines of the role he had played in bringing to national and international prominence the ministry of those who were being called the Kansas City Prophets. I was also very aware that, after a time, Wimber became disillusioned and all but repudiated prophetic ministry in general. However, I was unaware of the details of the unfolding situation, simply because, as it was happening, I was giving most of my time and attention to other priorities. Happily, these details are now thoroughly documented in Bill Jackson's work.

As I highlight some of these details, I want to be clear that I am not questioning in the least John Wimber's integrity as one of the outstanding Christian leaders of our generation. During his lifetime he probably influenced Christianity in the Anglo world (i.e., the United States, Canada, the United Kingdom, Australia, South Africa) and in other places as much as any other individual. But he also made his share of mistakes. Therefore, I can understand why God would suggest I review the history of the Association of Vineyard Churches, especially if it is God's desire that I receive any part of John's mantle for serving the prophetic movement (recognizing that this was only one of many mantles that John carried during his ministry).

The Need for Apostolic Leadership

If I were to reduce my fairly cursory historical analysis to one factor, in my opinion John Wimber's major shortcoming was his understandable reluctance at that time (i.e., the late '80s to mid-'90s) to recognize the contemporary gift and office of apostle. I interacted with John a great deal, during the months just preceding his death, both in personal conversation and by letter, on the issue of apostolic ministry. I actually felt he was moving in the direction of agreeing that this could be something the Spirit might now be saying to the churches, when he suddenly left us.

I also feel I should record the fact that when I heard John had died, it was the only time in my life I wept bitterly for someone who had just passed away, including the deaths of close relatives. It now appears obvious that God must have been saying something rather special.

I was interested to discover recently that others seem to be thinking along the same lines (regarding the need for greater recognition of the apostolic). Here is a quote from an excellent new book by British leader Peter Lyne, entitled *First Apostles, Last Apostles*:

> During a visit to California a few years ago, I took time to listen carefully to the teaching of some prominent leaders [of the movement of the Kansas City Prophets], and I visited a conference described as "A Gathering of Prophets" hosted by one of the main Vineyard churches. At that time, the thing that surprised me was the absence of any reference to the apostolic ministry, or if it was mentioned at all, it seemed to be merely an incidental. I commented to the American pastor I was travelling with that it seemed to me a particularly dangerous imbalance fraught with many pitfalls. Much of the teaching and prophetic ministry was sincere and commendable, but without the maturity of apostolic ministry alongside of it, it seemed particularly vulnerable. And so it has proved to be![4]

The History

For the purpose of this chapter, I am going to highlight several significant facts about John Wimber and the Kansas City Prophets found in Bill Jackson's *The Quest for the Radical Middle*. A good bit of this material will be my own paraphrase of what Jackson records, but for documentation I will insert page references to the facts I have in mind.

In the early 1980s, Mike Bickle planted a church in Kansas City called the Kansas City Fellowship. Over time it became the base of choice for the ministry of several individual prophets who desired to place themselves under the pastoral covering of Mike Bickle. This group grew to include such prophetic voices as Bob Jones, Paul Cain, John Paul Jackson, Jim Goll and many others. Some of the Kansas City folks had been attending Vineyard conferences from time to time, when, in October 1987, Bob Jones prophesied that a significant cross-pollination between Vineyard and Kansas City Fellowship would begin in January 1988. Sure enough, in January 1988, John Wimber suddenly felt impressed to call Mike Bickle, and the close association between the two groups began.[5]

The English Revival Disappointment

The friendship between Wimber and Bickle developed over the months, and then Paul Cain visited John in Anaheim, California, for the first time in December 1988. Several factors (including Cain's accurate prophecy about the earthquake, which I described in chapter 5) persuaded John that the Vineyard indeed needed to be more closely affiliated with the prophetic movement. John then felt led to invite Paul Cain into his inner circle.

A few months earlier, in August 1989 at a pastors conference in Denver, Cain called out pastors John and Eleanor Mumford of a Vineyard church in England and prophesied that major revival would break out in England in October.[6] When the next October came and went without revival, questions were raised. Someone pointed out that Paul Cain had not mentioned the *year*, so he was consulted and it seemed to all concerned that 1990, not 1989, would be the year when revival would break out in England in the month of October.[7]

By this time, Wimber had seen so many accurate prophecies fulfilled that he harbored no doubt the revival would come as prophesied. Thinking that October 1990 would likely mark a turning point with worldwide historic implications, John took his entire family, including his grandchildren, to England to witness this epochal event. However, when expectations were once again not realized, Wimber began to reconsider what he had done with the Kansas City Prophets.

The Ernie Gruen Controversy

Meanwhile, another severe complication had entered the picture. In January 1990, Ernie Gruen, an influential Kansas City pastor who had been building a case against the Kansas City Prophets for some time, finally went public with a recording of a sermon entitled "Do We Keep On Smiling and Say Nothing?" He proceeded to circulate thousands of copies of the audiotape through his worldwide mailing list.

Gruen followed this up in May with a 233-page criticism entitled "Documentation of the Aberrant Practices and Teachings of Kansas City Fellowship." This caused charismatic leaders across the country to begin taking sides. In an effort to manage the controversy and facilitate whatever damage control might be possible, John Wimber agreed to absorb Mike Bickle and the Kansas City Fellowship into the Association of Vineyard

Churches. Wimber then decided to deviate from his normal pattern of not responding to critics and to move into polemics.[8]

This controversy, combined with a similar attack from Australia and the disappointment over the prophesied—but unrealized—revival in England, was very draining on John. In May 1991 he used a meeting of the board of the Association of Vineyard Churches, held in Snoqualmie Falls, Washington, to begin a process of backing off on what had been perceived by some as unconditional support of the prophetic movement, represented by the Kansas City Prophets.

The phrase was used that Vineyard had to get "back on track" as a movement.[9] Bill Jackson reports that four years later at a pastors' conference in Anaheim Hills, California, in 1995, "Wimber told the movement that he regretted leading the Vineyard into the prophetic era, saying that it did, indeed, get [them] off track. Behind closed doors, it became apparent that John had been deeply hurt by the lack of a significant revival in London and had become disillusioned."[10]

WHAT CAN WE LEARN?

Again, I have recorded these facts not by way of criticism or reprimand but as an opportunity to learn from the past as we plan for the future. As I ask myself why the Lord prompted me to review the history of the Vineyard, I have concluded that there are several important lessons, at least for me, as I participate in what some might see as a newer phase of the prophetic movement. Keep in mind that my participation in the prophetic movement is not as a bona fide prophet, but only as an apostle. In my understanding, one of the principal responsibilities of an apostle is to bring order and an appropriate degree of structure to a movement, which I feel I should attempt to do. In all of this, I am very much aware of my personal limitations since I am but a beginner in providing apostolic leadership.

Here is what I think we can learn from the Vineyard/Kansas City Prophets experience:

1. Order Is Needed.

The prophetic movement has a felt need for order. This is one thing that had attracted the Prophets and their pastor, Mike Bickle, to John Wimber. The prophets who are members of the Apostolic Council of Prophetic Elders would affirm this.

2. Apostolic Leadership Is Required.

The order needs to be established by apostolic leadership. In the late 1980s the gift and office of apostle had not yet begun to be widely recognized by the Body of Christ. Nevertheless, in one of the earlier Vineyard pastors' conferences in which the prophets had a prominent role, Bill Jackson reports that it was prophesied:

> *The enemy had stolen the foundational ministries of the apostle and prophet from the church, but God was now restoring them. We were seeing the emergence of the prophetic in the '80s and they would come into maturity in the '90s. We would begin to see a new wave of apostolic men in the '90s who would come to maturity after the turn of the millennium.* [11]

3. Pastoring Is Not Apostling.

In my opinion, John Wimber was a true apostle and pioneer of what we now call the New Apostolic Reformation. It is totally understandable, however, that it would have been virtually impossible for him to publicly accept this potentially controversial role, given the several pressures he was experiencing at the time. His hands were so full of the prophetic that he would have had little surplus patience for the apostolic. One of the more revealing statements in Bill Jackson's book is this: "Bob Fulton [Wimber's brother-in-law and close confidant] told me that at this point [the board meeting in Snoqualmie Falls in 1991] John realized that he had been intimidated by the prophets' gifting, and he had not realized that he had the authority to *pastor* them."[12]

I italicized the verb "pastor" because I now believe that God's calling to John would not have been to *pastor* the prophets but rather to *apostle* the prophets.

4. Vertical Apostles Have Limitations.

Even if John had acknowledged his apostolic office, it might have been especially difficult for him to implement it because he was a *vertical* apostle, not a *horizontal* apostle. His primary apostolic sphere was the (vertical) Association of Vineyard Churches. In order for him to exercise authority over the Kansas City Prophets, he felt he had to incorporate them into his sphere and make them members of Vineyard. One of the implications of this action was that from that point onward, criticisms of the Prophets were, by virtue of association, implicitly directed against all members of Vineyard. This was unacceptable to some, and several pioneer AVC board members resigned.[13] It eventually became evident that such a relationship was dysfunctional. Wimber was buffeted with criticism regarding the whole Vineyard Movement that he founded. The criticism came from both within and without the movement. He finally succumbed and dissolved the relationship with the Kansas City Prophets.

MOVING ON

I currently see the Apostolic Council of Prophetic Elders (ACPE), led by a horizontal apostle, as a much more viable vehicle for bringing order to the prophetic movement than the experiment we have been analyzing. This is based on the principle of the differing functions of vertical and horizontal apostles which I explained in chapter 3. Bringing peer-level prophets together in ACPE requires a horizontal apostle like James of Jerusalem, who was not seen as *over* those we called together as a "covering." Vertical apostles, by definition, are *over* the members of their network. Horizontal apostles lead simply by convening.

Given the rapidly arising acceptance of prophets and prophetic ministries in general, it is my expectation that many councils of prophets like ACPE, by whatever name, will be emerging in the United States and around the world. Because a given apostle can relate effectively only to a limited number of prophets, I would expect the size of these units to run somewhere between 15 and 40 prophets each. My ideal number is 25.

This may or may not be what God has in mind. But if God does raise up several prophetic councils under apostolic leadership, it is conceivable that the apostles who moderate them will seek ways of building productive relationships with each other. This could become a vehicle for widespread coordination, accountability and heightened integrity within the prophetic movement in general.

THE TEST: PUBLIC ACCOUNTABILITY

How seriously are the prophets taking this expressed desire to test their prophecies with each other before they are announced, and their responsibility for them after they are announced?

I am glad to report that at least the members of the Apostolic Council of Prophetic Elders are very serious. On November 30, 1999, the day before the World Congress on Prayer and Intercession held in Colorado Springs, a meeting of the ACPE was held to discuss what the Lord seemed to be saying for the new millennium. The prophetic words were exchanged among those present, mutually judged and written in a document, "A Word upon Entering the New Millennium." During an evening plenary session of the conference, Cindy Jacobs called to the platform seven of the ACPE members who were present, including me. I explained to the audience what I have been trying to say in this chapter, namely, that there is a desire on the part of many prophets to hold themselves accountable to the public for their prophecies.

I then proceeded to read verbatim the prophecies that were issued from the meeting of ACPE on January 27, 1999, which had circulated widely through the media, and also from the current November 30 document. The January prophecies dealt with international alliances, Y2K, economic shakings, terrorism, Colorado Springs, humility, President Clinton and coming days of glory, stressing that prophecy is conditional and calling for fervent intercession. The November prophecies dealt with Russia (especially Russian Jews), a youth revival, a signs-and-wonders/evangelism movement, worship in stadiums, women, economic shakings, weather patterns, the apostles and prophets movement, holiness, international alliances and the northeast United States.

I read each prophecy from the past, which had been in the public domain for 10 months, and then each of the new ones. I paused after each prophecy, and Cindy Jacobs and different prophets standing on the platform made appropriate comments as the Lord directed. I believe this was a first, with a number of prophets, led by an apostle, standing before an audience of 1,500, holding themselves accountable—individually and collectively—to the wider Body of Christ. The spiritual impact was incredible, and I believe the prophetic movement has risen to a new level.

THE HARNESS MAKES ALL THE DIFFERENCE

By way of conclusion, let me flash back once more to the draft-horse pull. In one of the last heavyweight horse pulls that Doris and I attended, one of the traces on the harness, a leather strap connecting the horse collar to the whiffletree, snapped as the horses lurched forward to pull the sled. As a result, the team was automatically disqualified. For all we know, they could have been the two strongest draft horses in the nation, but they could not win the contest without a sound harness.

This is the same with apostles and prophets today. We cannot have the best possible foundation for the Church of the future unless we have genuine apostles and genuine prophets. But the gifts and the offices are not enough. It is only when apostles and prophets are properly harnessed and pulling together that the kingdom of God will advance throughout the world as God desires it to advance in our generation.

Notes

1. Ted Haggard, "Do the Prophets Really Know?" *Ministries Today,* March/April 1999, p. 25.
2. Chuck D. Pierce and Rebecca Wagner Sytsema, *Receiving the Word of the Lord* (Colorado Springs, CO: Wagner Publications, 1999), p. 30.
3. Ibid., pp. 31-36.
4. Peter Lyne, *First Apostles, Last Apostles* (Tonbridge, Kent, England: Sovereign World, 1999), p. 14.
5. Bill Jackson, *The Quest for the Radical Middle: A History of the Vineyard* (Cape Town, South Africa: Vineyard International Publishing, 1999), pp. 198-200.
6. Ibid., p. 208.
7. Ibid., pp. 209, 210.
8. Ibid., pp. 216-218.
9. Ibid., p. 229.
10. Ibid., p. 234.
11. Ibid., pp. 206, 207.
12. Ibid., p. 230.
13. Ibid., p. 232.

INDEX